C. C. Ranner

SELECTIONS FROM
LUCRETIUS

SELECTIONS FROM
LUCRETIUS

EDITED BY

G. E. BENFIELD, M.A.
Former Head of the Classics Department
Chippenham Grammar School

AND

R. C. REEVES, B.A.
Former Head of the Classics Department
Accrington High School

OXFORD UNIVERSITY PRESS

Oxford University Press, Walton Street, Oxford OX2 6DP

OXFORD   LONDON   GLASGOW
NEW YORK   TORONTO   MELBOURNE   WELLINGTON
IBADAN   NAIROBI   DAR ES SALAAM   CAPE TOWN
KUALA LUMPUR   SINGAPORE   JAKARTA   HONG KONG   TOKYO
DELHI   BOMBAY   CALCUTTA   MADRAS   KARACHI

The cover portrays the Venus Genetrix, an antique statue now in the Uffizi Gallery, Florence, against the background of atomic structure according to modern theory.

The epithet Genetrix was given because she was regarded as the mother of the gens Iulia and her worship under this title was an important part of the Imperial cult.

Mansell Collection

Printed and bound in Great Britain by
REDWOOD BURN LIMITED
Trowbridge & Esher

PREFACE

THIS book of selections springs from the belief, founded on experience, that intelligent post-'O'-level Latin students may obtain much profit and enjoyment from Lucretius. There is nothing surprising about this, because, unlike some more widely read Roman poets, Lucretius has something important to say and, at his best, says it with passion and precision. Like his master Epicurus Lucretius admitted that his work would never please the multitude. But the select company of pupils who do continue Latin after passing it at 'O' level are capable, in our view, of benefiting from Lucretius more than from any other Latin poet; always provided that they are given sufficient help with grammatical difficulties, that the most suitable passages are studied, and that the students are encouraged to link up the arguments of Lucretius with other subjects.

In this connexion we have an eye to a truly tormenting educational problem. Whatever be the value of Lord Snow's 'two culture' thesis outside the schools, it does seem true that much sixth form work is calculated to push ever farther apart two main groups of pupils, who have to equip themselves with the greatest possible haste to become specialists in either Arts or Science. Yet some Arts students we have known have read Lucretius' lucid exposition of the atomic theory and then been interested enough to pursue the historical changes it has undergone, and especially to learn what the modern nuclear physicist is doing. Similarly, there have been Science students who, though engaged in nothing more high-minded than 'keeping up their Latin', have come under the spell of Lucretius' skilled yet passionate poetry, and have been willing to investigate further what it is that poets, ancient and modern, are about.

These extracts are designed to show what Lucretius had to say and how he said it: hence the notes are not only grammatical but also cultural. Above all they are intended to present a poet who is also a thinker, prepared to argue his case by constantly appealing to reason. A distinguished modern poet and Professor of English Literature, William Empson, has said of his reaction to John Donne: 'We all said we admired him because he was so metaphysical, but I can see now that I really liked him because he argued.' Whatever teacher and pupil think of Lucretius' metaphysics, we believe both will find the study of him rewarding, for he is a great poet who argues.

CONTENTS

ACKNOWLEDGEMENTS AND NOTE ON THE TEXT

MUCH the largest debt we owe in preparing this selection from the *De Rerum Natura* is to the great edition of Cyril Bailey (Oxford, 1947), but we have also derived much valuable help from Sinker's *Introduction to Lucretius* (Cambridge, 1937), from the editions of Books I–III by Lee (Macmillan, 1893), of Book V by Duff (Cambridge, 1889) and of the latter half of Book V by Lowe (Oxford, 1907), and from the translations by Rouse (Loeb, 1937) and Latham (Penguin, 1951). For the treatment of Metre we are deeply indebted to C. G. Cooper's *An Introduction to the Latin Hexameter* (Macmillan, 1952).

We have adopted without exception, and largely without comment, Bailey's 1947 text. For the convenience of readers using the Oxford Classical Text, second edition (1921), we list below those places in this selection where, in the 1947 edition, Dr. Bailey departed from his earlier text. His own words[1] are: 'I have become more conservative in my views and more ready to place reliance on the Leyden MSS. as the result of further study of Lucretius' grammar and idiom. In the 149 places where I have made changes from the Oxford Classical Text of 1921, I have returned in 91 to the manuscript reading.'

Extract no.	*De Rerum Natura*	1947	1921
1	I. 17	rapacis	rapaces
6	I. 267	ne qua	nequa
6	I. 283	aquai,	aquai
6	I. 289	ruitque et quidquid	ruit †qua quidquid†
7	I. 942	valescat;	valescat,
8	II. 22	possint;	possint.
12	II. 356	quaerit	†non quit†

[1] Preface, p. viii.

Extract no.	De Rerum Natura	1947	1921
12	II. 358	querellis	querelis
16	III. 444	incohibens sit	†incohibescit†
19	III. 1011	Furiae	furiae
19	III. 1012	aestus,	aestus
19	III. 1012-3	*no lacuna indicated*	*lacuna indicated between these lines*
20	IV. 26-43	26-43	30-47
20	IV. 43	eorum	rerum (l. 47)
21	IV. 395	videtur	videntur
21	IV. 397	exstantis ... montis	exstantes ... montes
23	IV. 1022	exterruntur	exterrentur
24	V. 201	avidam	avide
24	V. 216	peremunt	perimunt
24	V. 230	loquella	loquela
25	V. 425	pertemptare	pertemptare,
26	V. 941	arbita	arbuta
26	V. 947	claricitat	claru' citat
26	V. 948	vagis	vagi
31	VI. 384	partim	partem
32	VI. 685	percitus, aer	percitus aer
32	VI. 702	nominitant, nos	nominitant; nos

Benfield + Reeves: Selections from Lucretius
pub 1967.

INTRODUCTION

If Leonardo da Vinci had composed a poem about his
scientific discoveries and speculations, if Tennyson had
devoted himself to expounding Darwin's *Origin of Species*, if
Dr. Bronowski were a poet or T. S. Eliot had had Lord
Snow's scientific background—then the uniqueness of
Lucretius' *De Rerum Natura* might by now have been
challenged. But, as it is, we must accept Aldous Huxley's
verdict: 'In Lucretius the passionate apprehension of ideas,
and the desire and ability to give them expression, combined
to produce that strange and beautiful epic of thought which
is without parallel in the whole history of literature.'

The ideas of the great philosophers of free Greece—
Socrates, Plato, and Aristotle—had little immediate influence
upon the Romans. The two principal philosophical systems
which rivalled each other in Roman thought, Stoicism and
Epicureanism, were first propounded at Athens by Zeno and
Epicurus respectively, both some forty years younger than
Aristotle, both in their infancy in 338 B.C. when Greece fell
to the Macedonian conqueror, and both preaching to a subject
people.

Only fragments survive of the thirty-seven books which
Epicurus wrote under the title 'About Nature' ($Περί Φύσεως$).
Our knowledge of Epicureanism therefore is mainly derived
from the work of his Roman disciple Titus Lucretius Carus,
who expounded Epicurus' doctrines in six books of Latin
verse, translating Epicurus' title into Latin as *De Rerum
Natura*.[1]

---

[1] *res* points to reality as we see it to exist in its outward and visible
form—'all the choir of heaven and furniture of earth'; *natura* denotes the
inner essence of which that reality is composed, i.e. atoms and space.

Of Lucretius himself we know practically nothing. Jerome's biographical note ('Titus Lucretius the poet was born in the year 94, and having been driven mad by a love potion wrote in his lucid intervals several books, which were edited by Cicero, and died by his own hand in the forty-fourth year of his age') is quite unreliable. We can reasonably assume that he belonged to the *gens Lucretia*, one of the oldest patrician clans at Rome, and that his lifetime corresponded roughly to the first half of the first century B.C. He addresses as an equal Gaius Memmius, a Roman of ancient and high-born family, to whom the poem is dedicated. Memmius was praetor in 58 B.C. and governor of Bithynia the year after.[1]

Donatus, in his life of Vergil, states that Lucretius died on the Ides of October 55 B.C., Vergil's sixteenth birthday. This is probably not very far from the truth; in one of the last lines which he wrote[2] Lucretius makes a reference to the climate of Britain, which suggests that he may just have read or heard a report of Caesar's visit to the island in August and September 55. It is clear that he died before completing the poem, for Book VI breaks off short in the middle of a description of an epidemic, and there are places in the earlier work where, as in the *Aeneid*, the lack of final revision is noticeable. A reference by Cicero in a letter written to his brother Quintus in February 54 (*Lucreti poemata ut scribis ita sunt—multis luminibus ingeni: multae tamen artis*)[3] indicates that both had read the poem, but whether in manuscript or after

---

[1] Memmius was not, it would seem, an ideal student of Epicureanism. After his political career had culminated in disgrace and exile, we learn from a letter of Cicero (*ad Fam.* XIII. 1. 1) that, having gained possession of the ground at Athens on which stood the ruins of Epicurus' house, he proceeded to pull them down in order to build his own residence. Catullus, who served on his staff in Bithynia, has left on record his intense dislike of the man (X, XXVIII).

[2] VI. 1106.   [3] *ad Q. Fr.* II. 9. 4.

publication, and whether one of them was in fact the editor, it is impossible to say.

Whether or not Vergil assumed the *toga virilis* on the day Lucretius died, it is beyond question that in thought, language, and metre, Vergil was more profoundly influenced by Lucretius than by any other writer. Numerous passages, especially in the *Georgics*, bear witness to this influence: one in particular[1] is almost certainly a direct reference to Lucretius:

> *Felix qui potuit rerum cognoscere causas,*
> *atque metus omnis et inexorabile fatum*
> *subiecit pedibus strepitumque Acherontis avari.*

Horace, an 'Epicurean' in the more popular and debased sense, probably alludes to him in the words:

> *Deos didici securum agere aevum.*[2]

Ovid's tribute is quite explicit:

> *Carmina sublimis tunc sunt peritura Lucreti*
> *exitio terras cum dabit una dies.*[3]

Passing references are also found in Tacitus, Quintilian, and Statius.

Of Lucretius' life and character then we know little, although what he wrote survives in full. Of his master Epicurus (341-270 B.C.) the works are almost entirely lost, but we have a very clear picture of the man. He was an Athenian by family and descent, though born on the island of Samos. His father was so poor that he was reduced to school-teaching—'one of the last shifts of impecuniosity in the ancient world'[4]—and Epicurus had to assist by mixing ink for his father's pupils.

It is related that Epicurus turned to philosophy at the

---

[1] *Georgics* II. 490-2.   [2] *Satires* I. 5. 101.
[3] *Amores* I. 15. 23-24.   [4] Wallace, *Epicureanism.*

early age of 14 as a result of his disgust for the schoolmasters who could not tell him the origin of chaos in Hesiod.[1] At the age of 30 he was teaching philosophy at Mytilene. Five years later, in 307, he came to Athens and bought the house where he was to teach for the next thirty years in undisturbed tranquillity and intimate fellowship with his school.

The aim of Epicurus' philosophy was to free men from fear, to liberate them from everything in themselves and in the world to which they might be enslaved, and to lead them to *ataraxia* (ἀταραξία) or tranquillity. Such tranquil happiness was the end of all teaching, all learning, and all life. Any study which did not contribute to that end was superfluous.

To one pupil he writes: 'Blest youth, set sail in your bark and flee from all culture', and to another: 'I congratulate you in that you have approached philosophy free from all contamination—that is, quite untaught.'

The one study which he considered it important to engage in was the study of Nature. For by that study he believed the true causes of things could be discovered and men freed from fear—especially the fear of divine activity in the world.

What then does the study of natural phenomena teach? What scientific creed can explain the universe and man's place in it? What principles can make sense of all the observed facts of nature and human life? Epicurus' explanation of ultimate reality can be summed up in the one word *materialism*. This means, in the strict sense, that every happening in the outer world of events or the inner world of man's consciousness is connected with some material change, and in principle can ultimately be explained in terms of matter.

The reader may be surprised to learn that this creed is ancient as well as modern, and that it describes not only an attitude to life but also an hypothesis concerning the ultimate nature of reality. Whether it is the most adequate hypothesis

[1] Diogenes Laertius X. 2, ll. 14–18 (O.C.T.).

must depend on patient and prolonged scientific investigation. But it is perhaps fair to say that there is rather less confidence now than in the last century that the physical sciences can provide a complete picture of reality.

Indeed the physical scientist today would say that his task is not to provide pictures of the universe, but to formulate laws concerning material phenomena. 'In the case of atomic phenomena,' says the mathematician Dirac, 'no mental picture can be expected to exist in the usual sense of the word *picture*, by which is meant a model functioning on essentially classical lines.' It will certainly be a long time before so complete a picture of the universe as that provided by Newtonian physics will be available, though the longing to discover the pre-established harmony will continue to inspire men of science.

But for Lucretius the complete picture of the stuff of the universe was there, provided by the philosophy of Epicurus. For, like most considerable philosophies, Epicureanism claimed to offer not only a way of life, but also an explanation of reality.

Epicurus' explanation of the universe starts from the basic assumption that there are only two realities—material bodies and empty space (*inane*[1]). That there are bodies we know from our senses; and there must be empty space for them to move in, or there would be no such thing as motion. According to Epicurus, all bodies are ultimately composed of indivisible particles of matter whose differences in shape, size, and weight cause the immense difference between objects as we actually see and experience them. He borrowed this explanation of the universe, with some alterations, from two Greek philosophers of the fifth century B.C., Leucippus and Democritus—though it must be admitted that he never fully acknowledged his indebtedness to Democritus, and

[1] See commentary on extract no. 9, p. 32.

of Leucippus he asserted that there was no such man! These philosophers were called 'atomists' because they first used the word atom to express the ultimate particles of matter which are, as the name suggests, indivisible and indestructible. The atoms were also, according to Leucippus and Democritus, infinite in shape and variety. (Here Epicurus differed, and asserted that the number of atomic shapes and sizes, though immensely great, was not infinite.) They moved ceaselessly in empty space, which was real, though incorporeal.

The atomists were thoroughgoing materialists. Democritus declared that thought was a physical process and that the soul like the body was composed of atoms. They were also strict determinists. According to Leucippus, 'Nothing happens for nothing, but everything from a ground and of necessity.' Here again we find an interesting divergence in the Epicurean system. For, though he was a materialist, Epicurus was emphatically not a determinist. It was chiefly in order to emphasize the freedom of the will as against their belief in the iron law of 'Necessity' that he daringly postulated a 'swerve'[1] among the atoms, a free and random movement which caused them occasionally and unpredictably to collide with each other and so form the complex masses from which everything in the world,[2] and indeed in the vast spaces of the universe where new worlds are forever coming into being, has been fashioned. Throughout the universe there runs a writ of unpredictable spontaneity, however slight.

This picture of reality propounded by the atomists and borrowed by Epicurus must strike us as being more like physics than philosophy. Certainly, the first Greek philoso-

---

[1] See commentary on extract no. 11, p. 36.

[2] Our 'world' (*mundus*) comprises the earth and all that can be seen from it—sun, moon, and stars—and is separated from other such worlds by spaces called *intermundia*.

phers, in the sixth century B.C., were chiefly interested in discovering the primal stuff (*physis*) of the universe, and were themselves called *physici*. The earliest of them, Thales of Miletus (fl. 586 B.C.), boldly proclaimed that this primal stuff was water. This hypothesis was less foolish than it sounds, since water exists in three different forms: as solid (ice), liquid, and gas (steam). The atomists, however, postulated atoms in space as the irreducible material from which the universe is formed. In our century the atom has been split, and 'space', in the sense in which the atomists, then Epicurus and Newton after them, used it, has been much modified since Einstein. The modern physicist postulates that where there is not matter there is still something physical, namely electromagnetic vibrations, and matter itself is no longer conceived of as hard lumps of unchanging substance. The primary stuff of the universe, for modern science, is energy itself.

But the clue to ultimate reality which Epicurus inherited from the atomists, and which Lucretius was so devotedly to expound, was that everything consists of atoms, including the human soul. This is made of very fine atoms, and at death the connexion between the soul- and body-atoms is broken and the light soul-atoms dispersed. To coin an aphorism by slightly adapting a phrase from the Funeral Service, we may say, 'Atoms thou art and unto atoms thou shalt return.' Indeed Epicurus, and Lucretius after him, wished to set men free from the fear of death, and they did so by proving that death is literally nothing and the mythical terrors of the under-world—'bogyman horrors' as MacNeice described them with reference to *Aeneid VI*—a complete delusion.

Fear of the gods themselves was coupled with this fear of death, and, for Lucretius, Epicurus deserved undying fame for having destroyed *religio*. They were not concerned to deny the existence of gods, since the divine images were, in some sense, perceived, and this indicated some underlying reality, however deluded men were in their interpretations of these perceptions. Thus Epicurus declares, 'Gods there are, since the knowledge of them is by clear vision',[1] while Lucretius explains at length how men's minds are visited, in sleep especially, by visions of the gods.[2] These visions, he explains, are caused by *simulacra*, emanations from the bodies of the gods, which are too fine to be observed by ordinary sense-perception, but none the less real. It is the popular conception of gods as powerful beings who are continually interfering in human affairs that both are concerned to refute. And Lucretius concentrates the resources of his irony to describe the monarch on his throne trembling in superstitious awe at the lightning, or the storm-tossed naval commander reacting to the situation in the same way as the ship's captain in Shakespeare's *Tempest:* 'All's lost—to prayers'.[3] The world is governed not by gods, say Epicurus and Lucretius, but by the orderly and inexorable procession of atoms in space. As to the gods, what makes them gods is the very fact of their complete detachment from the world.

It was in order to prove the detachment of the gods from the concerns of men and hence set men free to pursue the life of 'settled, sweet, Epicurean calm'—*ataraxia*—that Epicurus advocated the study of natural phenomena.

A man cannot dispel his fear concerning the most important matters if he does not know what is the nature of the universe, but accepts the truth of some mythical story. So without natural science it is impossible to attain to pleasure unalloyed.[4]

This pleasure was nothing shallow or ephemeral, and was certainly far removed from the implications of luxurious

---

[1] *Ep. ad Men.* 123.
[2] V. 1161 sqq. (extract no. 29).
[3] V. 1218 sqq.
[4] Diogenes Laertius X. 143.

gluttony which the word *epicurean* now suggests. It was a completely calm, desireless attitude, which could be gained only by understanding and accepting reality. This was the way to that independence, that 'self-sufficiency'—*autarkeia* (αὐτάρκεια)—which was the supreme end of human existence. Here are Epicurus' own words on the subject of pleasure:

When, therefore, we maintain that pleasure is the end, we do not mean the pleasures of profligates and those that consist in sensuality, as is supposed by some who either are ignorant or disagree with us or do not understand, but freedom from pain in the body and from trouble in the mind. For it is not continuous drinkings and revellings, nor the satisfaction of lusts, nor the enjoyment of fish and other luxuries of the wealthy table, which produce a pleasant life, but sober reasoning, searching out the motives for all choice and avoidance, and banishing mere opinions, to which are due the greatest disturbance of the spirit.[1]

Such are the principles of the Epicurean philosophy, which remained substantially unchanged for at least seven centuries after its founder's death. As late as the third and fourth centuries A.D. the Christian writers Dionysius and Lactantius were attacking Epicureanism as a dangerous rival to their faith.

Lucretius himself closely and carefully follows his master's teaching, with as much zeal for right exposition as any orthodox Marxist interpreting his master. Why then do we call his poem unique? Assuredly not because he thought of its subject-matter out of his own head: few great poets have done that—certainly not Sophocles, Shakespeare, or Racine. It is unique because through it Lucretius set out to indoctrinate men with the spirit of science as a means of understanding the universe and their own place in it.

In theory, of course, a poem could be written on any theme,

---

[1] *Ep. ad Men.* 131–2.

but in practice the number of themes chosen by poets has been remarkably small, and usually quite unconnected with science. This is partly because great scientists have been too devoted to their own work of discovery to have time left over for poetry or anything else. Thus Darwin lamented his loss of music owing to the absorbing demands of his biological investigation, and complained that he had become 'a machine for grinding out general laws'.

On the other hand, poets themselves have been too busy practising their own art to have time to learn much about the subject-matter of science from the inside. Our own Wordsworth was convinced that poets could and should adopt scientific themes, and expressed himself to this effect in the Preface to *Lyrical Ballads*. But he was careful to add that, first of all, these discoveries must become familiar and, even more important, be capable of arousing deep emotion in both the poet and his audience:

> The remotest discoveries of the chemist, botanist, mineralogist, will be as proper objects of the poet's art as any upon which he is now employed, if the time should ever come when these things shall be familiar to us, and the relations under which they are contemplated shall be manifestly and palpably material to us as enjoying and suffering human beings.

Poets have, for long enough, felt passionately about the moon conceived as a pale disk; none as yet has been moved to write about it in terms of space-flight. Perhaps we must wait for the first moon-landing to provide inspiration for such a poem.

Meanwhile this 'strange and beautiful epic of thought' stands alone. For through it there breathes a passion which other great poets have found in such enormous themes as love or death, but rarely, if ever, in science or philosophy. Is there, for example, anything outside the Old Testament to approach the power and passion with which Lucretius demolishes the superstitious 'religion' of his day in I. 62-101[1], with its tremendous climax: *tantum religio potuit suadere malorum*? The whole passage breathes the spirit of an Amos or an Isaiah demolishing the idolatries of their people with blistering scorn.

Indeed, one feels that Lucretius, though 'impersonal' in the sense that he has not allowed us to gain an adequate picture of his own personality through his poem, any more than Shakespeare has, is nevertheless a profoundly religious man. The positive expression of his own religious feeling is called forth by the sheer beauty and order of the universe. For him the heavens declare the glory, not of God, but of the mysterious law which is behind it all.

Einstein once said: 'You will hardly find one among the profounder sort of scientific minds without a peculiar religious feeling of his own. . . . His religious feeling takes the form of rapturous amazement at the harmony of the natural law.'[2] The words echo those of Lucretius himself: 'At this (i.e. the contemplation of the universe as revealed through the Epicurean system) I am seized with a divine delight and a shuddering awe, that by your power nature stands thus unveiled and made manifest in every part.'[3]

No one but Plato, and possibly Dante, has been so vehemently gripped by ideas and able to expound them with such art. That is why the expression of admiration by Aldous Huxley seems to us deserved, and to that expression we should like to add the judgement of the most recent translator of the *De Rerum Natura*, R. E. Latham, with the hope that the reader himself will be able to endorse it: 'There is no ancient writer who speaks more directly to the modern reader.'

[1] Extracts nos. 3 and 4.
[2] Quoted by H. E. Huntley, *The Faith of a Physicist*, p. 70.
[3] R. E. Latham's translation of III. 28–30 (extract no. 15).

STYLE, LANGUAGE, AND METRE

EPICURUS wrote in prose. Lucretius chose to pass on his doctrines to the Roman reader through the medium of verse, using the metre of Homer's *Iliad* and *Odyssey*, the epic hexameter. His motive for doing so, as he makes clear in extract no. 7, is to sweeten the 'medicine' of philosophy with the 'honey' of poetry. But the philosophic message is of prime importance: style, language, and metre are at the service of his thought.

It need hardly be said that, as well as depending upon the thought which they express, style, language, and metre are very greatly interdependent. In attempting to deal with them under separate headings, for ease of future reference, we shall be unable to avoid considerable overlapping.

I. STYLE

It was Ennius, the father of Roman poetry, who first moulded Latin verse to the Greek hexameter, in his historical epic, the *Annals*. Lucretius clearly admired Ennius and took him as a model. He writes: 'He first brought down from lovely Helicon a garland of evergreen leaf to sound and shine throughout the nations of Italy.'[1] What Lucretius did was to take this verse-form of Ennius, with all its roughness and naïveté, and render it flowing yet strong. For Ennius much of the time seems to be hammering his words into verse with little regard to shape or sound, so that his style is at best rugged, and at worst degenerates into ungainly roughness. Indeed, a later Roman critic, Quintilian, compared the *Annals* to a sacred grove of aged oaks which struck the senses

[1] I. 117–19.

with awe rather than with the charm of beauty. Like Ennius Lucretius consciously aims at a style that is solemn, archaic, and exalted, as opposed to a natural, ordinary, conversational tone. But the verse of Lucretius is, at its best and most characteristic, supple as well as solemn, controlled and effective where that of Ennius is over-emphatic or unsure.

Examples of Lucretius' use of archaic words and grammatical forms will be given under the heading of 'Language', but here may be mentioned the suppression of final -*s* (e.g. *omnibu'* I. 159, extract no. 5), which probably represents a normal colloquial pronunciation of the times. It is common in Ennius, less so in Lucretius, and not found in any of his successors. Cicero had used it in the verse which he published earlier in his life, but writing some time after Lucretius' death described the practice as 'rather countrified' (*subrusticum*).

Like Ennius Lucretius makes much use of alliteration and assonance. Bailey describes that of Ennius as being 'straightforward and simple-hearted, and occasionally so exaggerated as to be almost absurd'.[1] Lucretius can be simple-hearted in imitation of his admired predecessor, but generally his usage is much more subtle. See, for example, I. 271 and 285–6 (extract no. 6), where the *v* and *p* sounds are artfully and effectively interwoven to suggest, in the one case, the rushing wind, in the other, the onrush of a flooded river; or V. 950 (extract no. 26), where a gentler stream is pictured in the repetition of the 'liquid' consonant *l*. In IV 400 (extract no. 21) the harsh *c* sounds suggest the staggering of the giddy child, and a very fine example is the description of celestial phenomena in V. 1189–93 (extract no. 29), with its *m* and *n* sounds rising in a gradual crescendo to the climax of *murmura magna minarum.*

Tmesis—the separation of a word into two parts—is another device which Lucretius employs more freely than his

[1] *Prolegomena*, p. 148.

successors, while avoiding the crudity of Ennius, whose famous *saxo cere- comminuit -brum* produces an effect more comic than impressive.[1] Vergil would not have permitted himself Lucretius' *ordia prima* for *primordia* (IV. 28, extract no. 20) and *inque peditur* for *impediturque* (VI. 394, extract no. 31), but for the most part Lucretius confines himself to milder instances, such as *quae . . . cumque* (II. 21, extract no. 8) and *inter . . . iecta* (III. 860, extract no. 17).

Hypallage, or 'transferred epithet', is common in Lucretius, as in most Roman poets: e.g. *species verna diei* for *species verni diei*, 'the face of the spring day' (I. 10, extract no. 1); *impia rationis elementa* for *impiae rationis elementa*, 'the rudiments of an impious philosophy' (I. 81, extract no. 4), etc. More peculiar to Lucretius is his fondness for substituting an attribute of something for the thing itself: e.g. *venti vis* for *ventus* (I. 271, extract no. 6), *aquae natura* for *aqua* (I. 281, extract no. 6), *puerorum aetas* for *pueri* (I. 939, extract no. 7), etc. This is so common that Bailey refers to it as 'the Lucretian periphrasis'.

In considering any Latin poetry two important facts must always be remembered. First, the art of rhetoric was the chief part of a Roman's education, and this influenced verse style almost as much as prose style. Secondly, poetry, no less than oratory, was written to be spoken and heard. Like other Roman poets Lucretius employs these devices to give rhetorical force and grandeur to his verse. But by his own use of them he achieves a poetic manner which, while it makes no pretence to being spontaneous or 'natural', is nevertheless completely personal to himself and, in its combination of dignity with clarity, admirably suited to its theme.

---

[1] Cf. Samuel Butler (*Hudibras*, I. 3. 328–9);

> That old Pyg- (what d' y' call him) -malion
> That cut his mistress out of stone.

The milder kind of tmesis is also known in English, e.g. 'what man soever'.

II. LANGUAGE

One characteristic which markedly differentiates the language of Lucretius and his predecessors from that of later poets is the use of compound adjectives. Such adjectives— formed from two noun-, adjective-, or verb- roots, as opposed to prefix-compounds like *impius, dissimilis*—are not natural to Latin, but were freely coined by early poets in imitation of Greek originals. Ennius sometimes misuses them to the point of absurdity, as in the line *bellipotentes sunt magi' quam sapientipotentes*. But some of his compounds are much more felicitous: e.g. *suaviloquens*, which Lucretius also uses (I. 945, extract no. 7). Often Lucretius will compose his own: e.g. *naviger* and *frugiferens* (I. 3, extract no. 1). Nearly always they add weight and dignity to his verse; never do they topple over into grandiosity.

It is impossible to read many lines of Lucretius without being struck by his strong predilection for two types of noun derived from verbs: those of the 4th declension, and neuters ending in *-men*. Here, of course, metrical considerations cannot be excluded: e.g. the use of *offensus* for "collision" (II. 223, extract no. 11) is dictated by the fact that the normal word *offensĭō* is impossible in hexameter verse; and while the prose word *frāgmēntă* is not metrically impossible, Lucretius' *frāgmĭnă* gives him an extra short syllable—a commodity badly lacking to the Roman poet. Nevertheless there are other instances, unaffected by considerations of metre, which point merely to personal preferences on Lucretius' part. Some of these nouns Lucretius found already in use, others he coined himself. Of the latter some passed into the language, others—such as *mactatus* I. 99 (extract no. 4), *conciliatus* II. 134 (extract no. 10), *clinamen* II. 292 (see commentary on extract no. 11, p. 36), *auxiliatus* V. 1040 (extract no. 28), *documen* VI. 392 (extract no. 31)—did not outlive their inventor.

Lucretius' preference for archaic words and grammatical forms has already been mentioned. Here again the choice is sometimes dictated by metre: e.g. *irritāt* I. 70 (extract no. 3) for *irritavit*; *indugredi* I. 82 (extract no. 4) for the impossible *īngrĕdī*; *ībŭs* II. 88 (extract no. 9) for *ĭīs*; *cŭppēdō* III. 994 (extract no. 19) for *cŭpīdō*; *navita* V. 223 (extract no. 24) for *nauta*. But again it is not always so: older forms like *rursum* I. 57 (extract no. 2) and III. 1001 (extract no. 19), *reddunda* I. 59 (extract no. 2), *prorsum* II. 340 (extract no. 12), *experiundo* V. 428 (extract no. 25), *ollis* VI. 687 (extract no. 32) are preferred where *rursus*, *reddenda*, *prorsus*, *experiendo*, *illis* would scan equally well, so that solemnity of style must be the criterion. Similarly with Lucretius' use of 3rd conjugation forms of verbs which normally belong to a long-vowel conjugation, and less frequently the reverse: *cupĭret* I. 71 (extract no. 3) for *cupĕret*, *cōntŭĭmur* IV. 35 (extract no. 20) for *cōntŭēmur*, *lavĕre* V. 950 (extract no. 26) for *lavāre* and *scatĕre* V. 952 (extract no. 26) for *scatēre* can be attributed to the exigencies of metre, but not *exterruntur* IV. 1022 (extract no. 23) for *exterrentur*.

Other archaisms which Lucretius frequently uses are the ending *-ier* instead of *-i* in passive and deponent present infinitives, and *-ībam* instead of *-iebam* in 4th conjugation imperfect indicatives. Another is the disyllabic ending *-āī* instead of the monosyllabic *-āe* for the 1st declension genitive singular. Originally the genitive singular of 1st declension feminine nouns ended in *-ās* (which survived into classical Latin in *pater familias* and similar phrases), and of masculine nouns in *-āī* (formed by adding the 2nd declension *-i* to the *-a-* of the 1st declension stem). Later *-ai* superseded *-as* in feminine nouns also, and finally was modified to *-ae*.

Before leaving the topic of Lucretius' use of language, we

should notice his resourcefulness. There was no philosophic or scientific vocabulary available to him in Latin, and so he was compelled to create his own. This he achieves with originality and poetic power. For example, he is nowhere content to transliterate the Greek word for 'atoms'—*atomoi* (ἄτομοι)—but instead uses the novel and expressive word *primordia*, or (for the genitive and ablative, since those of *primordia* are metrically impossible) *principia*, together with the interesting and colourful synonyms which he lists in I. 58–61 (extract no. 2). In non-technical vocabulary he is no less enterprising, and does not hesitate to coin a new word or form when his purpose requires it: thus when he wants a synonym for *catulus*, the Greek word *scymnus* appears for the first and only time in Latin (V. 1036, extract no. 28), while his *alituum* for the less tractable *ālĭtum* as the genitive plural of *ales* (V. 1039, extract no. 28) was found useful by several later poets.

III. METRE

We assume that the reader is already familiar with the general rules of prosody and with the scheme of the epic hexameter, and shall confine ourselves therefore to a few special points which may be found helpful.

It is a source of confusion that the same terminology ('long' and 'short') and the same symbols (— and ◡) are conventionally used to distinguish both different kinds of vowel and different kinds of syllable. We can only hope that when the reader saw *cōntŭĭmur* so printed (p. xxvii), he understood the long-quantity mark to refer to the syllable over which it is placed, not to the vowel, which is short; but that when, in the note on III. 993 (extract no. 19), he sees *exēst*, he will realize that this time we are drawing attention to the length of the vowel: *est* is always a long syllable, but the *e* is short if it comes from *sum*, long if it comes from *edo*.

Until different terms and symbols are generally accepted, the distinction cannot be made clear.

The first two syllables of *fragmenta* are long in spite of containing short vowels because they are closed syllables: i.e. when the word is correctly divided into its syllables—*frag-men-ta*—they end in consonants. A syllable is only short if it contains a short vowel *and* is an open syllable—i.e. ends in a vowel, though it may be open as the result of liaison of a final consonant with a following word beginning with a vowel: e.g. *gĕ-nŭ-s ōm-ne* I. 4 (extract no. 1).

It must be remembered that *h* is always negligible in scansion and should be bracketed as a reminder of that fact, and that *x* is itself a double consonant and, when followed by a vowel, should be written *c-s:* e.g. *gĕ-nĕ-trīc-s (h)ŏ-mĭ-nūm*.

There are a few cases where it is less obvious that two consonants were pronounced, though only one appears in the conventional spelling of the word, so that the preceding syllable is closed and therefore long, even if it contains a short vowel:

1. In present-stem forms of compounds of *iacio* a consonant *i* was pronounced before the vowel *i* which represents the *a* of the simple verb: e.g. *conicio* was pronounced *con-ji-ci-o*.

2. Consonant *i* between two vowels was pronounced double: e.g. *Graius* as *Graj-jus*, *cuius* as *cuj-jus*, *maior* as *maj-jor*, *aiunt* as *aj-junt*.

3. The *l* in *religio* was pronounced double: *rel-li-gi-o*.

4. The *c* in *hoc* (nominative and accusative neuter, in which the *o* is short) was pronounced double, the word being a contraction of *hodce*: e.g. III. 1000 (extract no. 19) *(h)oc-c es-t ạd-ver-so* etc.

5. The same usually applies to *hic* (the pronoun, in which the *i* is short, whereas it is long in the adverb): e.g. II. 132 (extract no. 10) *sci-li-ce-t (h)ic-ç ạ* etc. This is due to false analogy with *hoc*, *hic* being a contraction of *hice*.

The word *pĕrăgro* is so printed in Lewis and Short. This means that the *a* is short, but the second syllable may be short or long according to whether the word is pronounced *pe-ra-gro* or *pe-rag-ro*. The former should be regarded as normal (as in English we say *a-gree*, not *ag-ree*), the latter as abnormal, though by no means uncommon as a way out of a metrical difficulty. The same applies to any word in which a short vowel is followed by a combination of a mute (*b, c, d, f, g, p,* or *t*) and a liquid (*l* or *r*). The mute does, however, always end the syllable if it is the last letter of a preposition-prefix: e.g. *sub-la-ta*. This does not mean, of course, that a preposition-prefix is to be separated from the rest of the word when it is followed by a vowel: *subeo, adhibeo* are divided *su-be-o, a-d(h)i-be-o*.

Like other poets Lucretius frequently shortens a word by one syllable, either by syncope (the omission of a vowel between consonants) or by synizesis (the running together into one long vowel-sound of two vowels normally pronounced separately). Examples of syncope are: *saeclum* for *saeculum* I. 20 (extract no. 1) *et passim*; *periclum* for *periculum* II. 16 (extract no. 8) *et saepe*; *postus* for *positus* I. 52 (extract no. 2) and III. 857 (extract no. 17). Examples of synizesis are: *dēīn-de* I. 933 (extract no. 7) *et saepe*; *dēōr-sum* II. 217 and 221 (extract no. 11), but normally *dĕ-or-sum* III. 1016 (extract no. 19); *dēīn-ceps* II. 333 (extract no. 12); *an-tēāc-to* III. 832 and *dēēr-ra-runt* III. 861 (extract no. 17); *prōīn-de* IV. 386 (extract no. 21); *quōād* V. 1033 (extract no. 28). The spellings *prōbet* for *prŏhĭbet* III. 864 (extract no. 17) and *vēmenter* for *vĕhĕmenter* IV. 29 (extract no. 20) are also instances of synizesis, and a more extreme case is the scansion of *cuıus* I. 149 (extract no. 5) as one long syllable, the *i* (normally pronounced as a double consonant, as explained above) being vocalized and the three vowels run together.

Another metrical licence which Lucretius sometimes uses

is the interchange of vowel *u* and consonant *u*. Here the reader must not allow the conventional spelling in the text to obscure two facts: (i) the letter *v* was unknown to the Romans, who used *u* as both vowel and consonant; (ii) the *u* following *q* and sometimes *g* and *s* is just as much a consonant as the *u* which we print as *v*. Thus the conventional *suavis* is quite illogical: it ought to be either *suauis* or, to indicate its pronunciation, *svavis*. Instances of interchange are: *su-e-mus* for the normal *sve-mus* I. 60 (extract no. 2), *dis-so-lu-ant* for *dis-sol-vant* III. 903 (extract no. 18), and conversely *suo* scanned *svo* instead of *su-o* V. 420 (extract no. 25).

Latin, like English, has a stress-accent: i.e. in a word of two or more syllables one syllable is stressed more than the others. In Latin almost all words of two syllables are stressed on the first: words of three or more syllables are stressed on the penultimate syllable if it is long (e.g. *a-mà-bo, ma-gìs-ter*), but if that syllable is short, on the one before it (e.g. *mù-lĭ-er mu-lĭ-ĕ-rem, mu-li-ĕ-rĭ-bus*). Greek has not a stress-accent: consequently the adaptation to Latin of Greek metres set Roman poets a problem which had not arisen in Greek. In a 'falling' (i.e. dactylic or trochaic) metre there is a natural tendency to accent the first syllable of each foot: this is comparable to the 'beat' in music, and is called *ictus*:

> *Aéneadúm genetríx, hominúm divúmque volúptas.*

Should the poet try to arrange his line so that word-stress coincided with ictus or not? Ennius had no clear policy: his lines vary from complete coincidence through every kind of mixture to almost complete clash. It is in the verse of Cicero and Lucretius that we begin to find the pattern upon which Vergil was to set his seal—that of clash in the first part of the line and coincidence at the end:

> *Aénèadúm gènetríx, hòminúm divúmque volúptas.*

The effect is produced of a conflict between words and metre which is harmoniously resolved before the line comes to an end.

But it must not be thought that the pattern of clash and coincidence exemplified in the first line of the *De Rerum Natura*, which we have quoted, will be found in every line. The verse would become very monotonous if it were so. In fact the pattern is seldom the same in any two consecutive lines, and it is this constantly varying interplay between word-stress and ictus which gives the Latin hexameter its subtle and distinctive music. In the first three feet the practice of Lucretius and of later poets is similar: clash and coincidence are about equally common in the first, while in the second and third clash is the rule, coincidence exceptional. In the fourth foot Lucretius generally prefers coincidence, and has a marked liking for a single spondaic word in this position, whereas Vergil and his successors more often preferred to continue the conflict here.

It is in the last two feet, however, that the pattern is most stable in Lucretius and all subsequent users of the metre. Coincidence is almost invariable, and the occasional departure from it, by its ve~~ry rarity~~, becomes a useful device for the poet to heighten the emphasis, excitement, or grandeur of his line.[1] There are instances in Lucretius which appear to be dictated by mere metrical convenience, the more so as the nature of his subject-matter often necessitates the ending of a line with *res* or ~~*vis*;~~ but in others a deliberate effect is undoubtedly aimed at. In Book I there are two instances involving the word *cor*: *cŏrda tùá vì* 13 (extract no. 1) and *măgna mèúm còr* 923 (extract no. 7). Can we not hear the quickened heartbeat which is implied in the meaning of both lines? In *nŭlla quìés èst* II. 95 (extract no. 9) the restlessness of the atoms is reflected in the rhythm. In *aéthèriús sòl* V. 215

[1] Or even to produce deliberate bathos as in Horace's well-known *rìdìculús mùs*, *Ars Poetica* 139.

(extract no. 22) the emphasis thrown on to the final mono-syllable produces an impressive effect which Vergil copied several times.[1]

Finally, we must mention a practice frequently followed by both Ennius and Lucretius, but very rarely by later poets: that of filling the fifth and sixth feet with a single word of five syllables—or, if the fifth foot is a spondee, of four syllables: e.g. *religione* I. 63 (extract no. 3), *usurpare* I. 60 (extract no. 2). Not uncommonly it is a compound adjective which performs this function: e.g. *frugiferentis* I. 3 (extract no. 1), *suaviloquenti* I. 945 (extract no. 7).

Translation and scansion cannot be regarded as two separate and independent processes. Very often the second provides a valuable clue to the first. But we strongly urge that, when the meaning of a passage is fully understood, our appreciation of it will still be incomplete if we do not follow the Roman practice of reading it aloud. It is the union of sense and sound which makes poetry the supreme literary form.

[1] e.g. *Aeneid* I. 65, 105, III. 12.

LIST OF SELECTED PASSAGES

BOOK I

THIS book shows Lucretius as a man with a mission, and that mission is twofold. He seeks, first, to refute religion's claim to explain reality and rule men's destiny; second, to set up in its place the philosophy of Epicurus, which can do both these things because it is based firmly on the investigation of the real nature of things: that is, on physical science. This twofold task is reflected in the following extracts. Apart from the opening Invocation, three passages attack religion with prophetic vigour and scorn, while three lay the foundations of the physical explanation of the universe as propounded by Epicurus. We have not included the many other passages in which Lucretius criticizes rival theories, because, though interesting, these require a knowledge of some ancient philosophies which seem of slight relevance today, whereas the central question posed by this book—'Can religion be replaced by science?'—is as crucial now as then.

Before attempting an answer to this large question, we must outline an interesting historical problem which arises. Why did Lucretius need to attack religion, since no one of any consequence believed in it, certainly not the select audience to which he was deliberately addressing himself? Why expend so much energy in flogging a dead horse? To sharpen the problem, let us go back to the message and background of Epicurus himself. He sought to persuade his contemporaries in the Greek world of the third century B.C. not to believe in the intervention of the gods in human affairs. Such belief was irrational, he considered, because the explanation of events lies solely in the physical nature of the universe. More importantly such belief, he held, was immensely harmful, since it made men cower and grovel under the need to placate those capricious divine beings who might at any time destroy him. Life, in any case, was precarious enough for Epicurus' fellow-countrymen in the Greek city-states, which were under Macedonian domination. Sudden destruction might come, not from the gods, but from a marauding Macedonian army. The intervention of those all too human gods of Homer (still, at this time, the 'Bible of the Greeks') was so much a reflection of the earthly disorder in third-century Greece, that we can understand how much men needed to be freed from both.

There was an even darker side to religion, too. At the best the gods were capricious; at worst they could demand human sacrifice, as extract no. 4 shows. Throughout the barbarian world in Epicurus' time such human sacrifice was recognized. And in popular Greek religion it is now known that there was much superstition and cruelty. Modern research presents a very different picture from the sunny, romantic festival of Keats's *Ode on a Grecian Urn*, and reveals a dark underworld of magic and superstition. Epicurus himself was not of noble birth, and may well have had first-hand knowledge, not only of the Olympian religion, but also of the debased, popular superstition. His hostility to it is understandable and commendable.

But Lucretius' position and background seem widely different. For one thing, he was an aristocrat, standing apart from common life and religion. Incidentally, his age, unlike that of Epicurus, was not one of weariness in which men sought refuge from intolerable ills; men of titanic energy like Pompey and Caesar were carving out a name for themselves and changing the world. And we do not receive the impression that the scramble for power and plunder filled many of Lucretius' contemporaries with personal disillusionment. More importantly religion had no hold of any sort on the people to whom Lucretius addressed his burning words. Roman religion had never been very profound, though in the early days, no doubt, it was suited to the simple, hard-working Roman farmer, who believed that the earth was peopled with forces which had to be respected and placated by the proper observances and sacrifices. For the rest, religion was a practical matter of gaining material benefit or of avoiding calamity. The later developed religion of temple and priests, coupled with the imported Greek pantheon, was never very important, and, in Lucretius' time, scarcely more than a very minor department of state. The decay of public religion was symbolized by the physical decay of the temple buildings, which languished unrepaired.

The contemporary of Lucretius about whom we know most is Cicero, and his attitude to religion is significant. To be sure, he does retain the conventional language of belief in the gods in some speeches, and in his *De Legibus* prescribes the sort of religious observance he would like to see in a reformed republic: 'So in the very beginning we must persuade our citizens that the gods are the lords and rulers of all things, and that what is done, is done by their will and authority; that they are likewise great benefactors of men, observing the character of every individual, what he does, of what wrong he is guilty, and with what intentions and with what piety he fulfils his religious duties; and that they take note of the pious and the impious.'[1] But it will be obvious to any reader of Cicero's letters that the nature of the gods is of little concern to Cicero and his friends in their serious thinking, still less in the practical business of life.

State religion at this time was an empty shell, a minor device of party politicians. It was used by Bibulus in 59 B.C. in an attempt to invalidate the legislation of Caesar, his colleague in the consulship, and by Marcus Antonius in 44 B.C. to prevent the election of Dolabella. In view of Caesar's well-known pooh-poohing of the omens on the Ides of March, we can be sure that his eagerness to become *pontifex maximus* earlier in his career—so great that he is said to have told his mother, as he kissed her goodbye on the morning of the elections, that he would come home *pontifex maximus* or not at all—sprang more from ambition than from piety.

For common people the place of the official religion had been taken by the exotic and emotional cults from the East that came into the country with Rome's conquests, e.g. that of the Great Mother, which Lucretius himself refers to.[2] For the upper classes religion was replaced by the various brands of Greek philosophy,

---

[1] Cic. *De Leg.* II. 15. *sit igitur hoc iam a principio persuasum civibus, dominos esse omnium rerum ac moderatores deos, eaque, quae gerantur, eorum geri iudicio ac numine, eosdemque optime de genere hominum mereri et, qualis quisque sit, quid agat, quid in se admittat, qua mente, qua pietate colat religiones, intueri piorumque et impiorum habere rationem.* The translation is that of C. W. Keyes in the Loeb edition.

[2] II. 598 sqq. (extract no. 13).

notably Epicureanism, Stoicism, and Scepticism. The famous lawyer Scaevola summed up the attitude of the Roman upper classes to religion, when he said that a man had three creeds: one of outward ritual, which was part of the business of State; one which contained the accepted doctrines as to the gods and a future life, which was held only for the sake of imposing on the multitude; and his own real creed, which ignored the gods altogether, and contained only the teachings of philosophy.[1] A generation later Ovid wrote: *expedit esse deos, et, ut expedit, esse putemus.*[2]

Since those of Lucretius' contemporaries who were likely to read his work had no use for religion, is there not something incongruous about his attack, as though one were to lecture the Royal Society on the falsity of the belief in a flat earth? Lucretius may be determined to reproduce Epicurus' attitude to religion out of devotion to his master and the general principles he had laid down, in just the same way as a sincere middle-class Socialist might sing the 'Red Flag' while reflecting that the situation had changed a good deal since the days of Keir Hardie. The reader will judge whether this is a likely explanation.

Another is that Lucretius 'doth protest too much' against religion, because he is himself in need of his own exhortations, having felt within him the power even of a debased religion. This is a much more difficult thesis either to prove or to disprove, for who can know a man's real religious experience? Cyril Bailey affirms: 'The Roman, even in the most sceptical days, never quite lost the sense of a spiritual presence, which is the first essential of a religious consciousness.'[3] If beneath the surface of his own rational thought Lucretius felt the pull of the mysterious power that the early Romans had called *numen*, then we can perhaps understand his vehemence. But for whatever reason Lucretius turns aside again and again to assert the absolute supremacy of natural law over divine interference, to muster all his power of scorn and invective against a theological view of the universe.

Was he right to attack religion? The religious man, at any rate, will answer yes. This is exactly what those religious geniuses, the Hebrew prophets, did from the eighth to the sixth centuries B.C., with beneficial results to religion.[1] This is how progress in religion must come, however rudely disturbing it may seem to the 'believer' or idol-worshipper at the time. A. N. Whitehead made this point when he declared: 'Progress in religion is defined by the denunciation of gods. The key-note of idolatry is contentment with prevalent gods.'[2] The same point is being made even within established religion today, by such radical theologians as Bishop John Robinson. But it was the Lutheran pastor, Dietrich Bonhoeffer, who expressed it most starkly in his concept of 'religionless Christianity'. In the poignant *Letters and Papers from Prison*,[3] written before he was executed by the Nazis, he wrote: 'Our coming of age forces us to a true recognition of our situation vis-à-vis God, in that God is teaching us that we must live as men who can get along very well without him.' Epicurus and Lucretius would assuredly not have disagreed with that.

But can we go farther, and contemplate the actual replacement of religion by science? Only if science can provide men with the three fundamental needs of the spirit with which religion has been concerned. First, religion has supplied men with a philosophy, an explanation of the universe and of human life, however inadequate, or even fantastic. It is certainly possible to conceive of science taking over this aspect of religion, especially if we accept the magisterial dictum of Lord Russell: 'Whatever knowledge is attainable must be attainable by scientific methods; and what science cannot discover, mankind cannot know.'[4] Some would protest that this is unduly to limit the sphere of knowledge, and certainly the words have all the dogmatism of the famous aphorism fathered upon Benjamin Jowett:

> I am the Master of this college:
> What I don't know isn't knowledge.

Nevertheless any religion which claims to give a description or explanation of reality must come to terms with science. And if its

[1] See commentary on extract no. 3, p. 14.
[2] *Adventures of Ideas*, p. 17.
[3] p. 163.   [4] Bertrand Russell, *Religion and Science*, p. 243.

description will not stand up to scientific investigation, it is not likely to command the respect or adherence of men for long.

Secondly, religion has provided men with a scale of values, a code of behaviour, an answer to the question *What ought I to do?* Here again, vigorous take-over bids are being made by some scientists. Professor C. H. Waddington writes: 'Science itself, and, as far as I can see, only science by itself, unadulterated with any contrary ideal, is able to provide a way of life which is, firstly, self-consistent and harmonious, and, secondly, is free for the exercise of that objective reason on which our civilization depends.'[1] And Dr. Bronowski is equally categorical: 'We need an ethic which is moral and which works. It is often said that science has destroyed our values and put nothing in their place. . . . I believe that science can create values. . . . Science will create values, I believe, and discover virtues, when it looks into man; when it explores what makes him man and not an animal, and what makes his societies human and not animal packs.'[2] As in the first case, so here. Whether science takes over ethics from religion or not, it is unlikely that any code of behaviour will be widely accepted unless it can be shown to confirm those insights into human behaviour which are being slowly revealed to psychology and the social sciences.

So far, then, it is possible to contemplate with Lucretius the replacement of religion by science both as philosophy and as ethics. But man is not only a being who thinks and acts; above all, he feels. Philosophy may appeal to his intellect, ethics to the will, but it is the emotions which are basic. 'The intellect by itself moves nothing', said Aristotle;[3] 'feeling is all', affirmed Goethe,[4] and the profounder students of human nature have agreed. Man needs, it would seem, not only to describe and analyse reality with his head, but to commune with it in his heart, and through that communion to find peace. From the savage dancing round his totem pole to the Quaker sitting in silent worship religion has meant this.

---

[1] *The Scientific Attitude*, p. 124.
[2] *The Common Sense of Science*, p. 153.
[3] διάνοια δ' αὐτὴ οὐθὲν κινεῖ, *Nicomachean Ethics* 6. 2. 5.
[4] 'Gefühl ist alles', *Faust*, Part I, Scene 16, l. 48.

'Some in one way, and some in others, we seem to touch and have communion with what is beyond the visible world. In various manners we find something higher, which both supports and humbles, both chastens and transports us.'[1]

The activity in which the scientist is engaged is essentially impersonal: his relationship with the object is *I-it*. When that activity becomes personal, and the relationship is *I-thou*, science has been left behind. A scientist, be he physicist or psychologist, who becomes emotionally involved with his 'object', has ceased to be scientific about it. This may happen when scientific thought or discovery itself leads on to rapture.[2] Again, the scientist—or anyone else!—may fall in love, or undergo the sort of mystical experience which befell Wordsworth when he gazed at the majestic scenery above Tintern Abbey, and felt

> that serene and blessed mood
> In which the burthen and the mystery
> Of all this unintelligible world
> Is lightened.

This is the religious experience in essence. It is not the analytic, scientific knowledge which Lucretius describes as learning 'to see in what pattern the whole universe stands framed';[3] yet, at its highest, it does lead the worshipper, as Wordsworth went on to say, 'to see into the life of things'.

1. Invocation to Venus, the Creative Power of Nature

(I. 1–25)

The poet calls on Venus, the mother of the Roman race, the mysterious power also that fills the universe, creating and directing all things with ceaseless, inexhaustible energy, as he sets out on his task of explaining the nature of things:

'Life-giving Venus, at your coming winds and clouds depart,

[1] F. H. Bradley, quoted by C. A. Coulson, *Science and Christian Belief*, p. 141.

[2] See Introduction, p. xxi, and note to III. 28, extract no. 15.

[3] I. 950 (extract no. 7).

the earth puts forth flowers, sea and sky smile. Birds and beasts welcome you. You inspire love in the hearts of all creatures and lead them to propagate their species. Queen of nature, aid me in my task of writing on nature.'

Opposite the text are four stanzas of Spenser's *Faerie Queene*,[1] one of the many adaptations which this passage has inspired.

Aeneadum genetrix, hominum divumque voluptas,
alma Venus, caeli subter labentia signa
quae mare navigerum, quae terras frugiferentis
concelebras, per te quoniam genus omne animantum
concipitur visitque exortum lumina solis: 5
te, dea, te fugiunt venti, te nubila caeli
adventumque tuum, tibi suavis daedala tellus
summittit flores, tibi rident aequora ponti
placatumque nitet diffuso lumine caelum.
nam simul ac species patefactast verna diei   10
et reserata viget genitabilis aura favoni,
aeriae primum volucres te, diva, tuumque
significant initum perculsae corda tua vi.
inde ferae pecudes persultant pabula laeta
et rapidos tranant amnis: ita capta lepore   15
te sequitur cupide quo quamque inducere pergis.
denique per maria ac montis fluviosque rapacis
frondiferasque domos avium camposque virentis
omnibus incutiens blandum per pectora amorem
efficis ut cupide generatim saecla propagent.   20
quae quoniam rerum naturam sola gubernas
nec sine te quicquam dias in luminis oras
exoritur neque fit laetum neque amabile quicquam,
te sociam studeo scribendis versibus esse
quos ego de rerum natura pangere conor.   25

[1] Book IV, Canto X, 44–47.

Great Venus, Queene of beautie and of grace,
  The joy of Gods and men, that under skie
  Doest fayrest shine, and most adorne thy place,
  That with thy smyling looke doest pacifie
  The raging seas, and makst the stormes to flie;
  Thee goddesse, thee the winds, the clouds doe feare,
  And when thou spredst thy mantle forth on hie,
  The waters play and pleasant lands appeare,
And heavens laugh, and al the world shews joyous cheare.

Then doth the daedale earth thraw forth to thee
  Out of her fruitfull lap aboundant flowres,
  And then all living wights, soone as they see
  The spring breake forth out of his lusty bowres,
  They all doe learne to play the Paramours;
  First doe the merry birds, thy prety pages
  Privily pricked with thy lustfull powres,
  Chirpe loud to thee out of their leavy cages,
And thee their mother call to coole their kindly rages.

Then doe the salvage beasts begin to play
  Their pleasant friskes, and loath their wonted food;
  The Lyons rore, the Tygres loudly bray,
  The raging Buls rebellow through the wood,
  And breaking forth, dare tempt the deepest flood,
  To come where thou doest draw them with desire:
  So all things else, that nourish vitall blood,
  Soone as with fury thou doest them inspire,
In generation seeke to quench their inward fire.

So all the world by thee at first was made,
  And dayly yet thou doest the same repayre:
  Ne ought on earth that merry is and glad,
  Ne ought on earth that lovely is and fayre,
  But thou the same for pleasure didst prepayre.
  Thou art the root of all that joyous is,
  Great God of men and women, queene of th' ayre,
  Mother of laughter, and welspring of blisse,
O graunt that of my love at last I may not misse.

This invocation to Venus has caused much perplexity to readers and even more argument among scholars. For one who aims to free men from the fear of gods by proving that they are entirely separate from and indifferent to the life of this world, it seems strangely inconsistent to begin with a prayer to a particular divinity. Of the many explanations given we single out three:

1. It has been a habit of poets to invoke the Muses at the beginning of their work. So Homer begins the *Iliad*, 'Sing, O goddess...'. In this purely conventional fashion Lucretius himself later[1] invokes the Muse Calliope. Elsewhere[2] he says that it is permissible to 'abuse' the names of Neptune, Ceres, and Bacchus for 'sea', 'corn', and 'wine', provided that the mind remains untouched by superstition, and in fact he several times[3] avails himself of this convention of poetic diction. Somewhat similarly, he calls the woods 'the haunts of the nymphs',[4] and in the present passage uses the term 'unbarred'[5] of the wind, as if in reference to the myth that the winds were kept imprisoned in the cave of Aeolus.

2. But this is much more than a conventional address. There is an unmistakable earnestness coupled with its beauty. It is not just a particular goddess, but the whole creative power of nature, the 'life force' which sustains all things, that Lucretius here invokes. So Tennyson, in his *Lucretius*,[6] makes the poet say:

> Ay, but I meant not thee; I meant not her,
> Whom all the pines of Ida shook to see
> Slide from that quiet heaven of hers, and tempt
> The Trojan, while his neat-herds were abroad.
> .   .   .   .   .   . Rather, O ye gods,
> .   .   .   . did I take
> That popular name of thine to shadow forth
> The all-generating powers and genial heat
> Of Nature . . . .

---

[1] VI. 94.   [2] II. 655–60 (extract no. 14).
[3] Neptune = sea, II. 472 and VI. 1076; Bacchus = wine, III. 221. Venus = love, V. 1017 (extract no. 27).   [4] V. 948–9 (extract no. 26).
[5] *reserata* 11.   [6] Lines 85–88, 92, 95–98.

So also a modern admirer of Lucretius, Miss Brigid Brophy, writes: 'The artist, too, has to invoke a power of whose origin his conscious mind knows nothing, and which he therefore images to himself as a visitor from outside. Lucretius's scientific imagination has led him to go on from biology to psychology; he possesses a shrewd insight into the nature of the poet's unconscious inspiration, and seeks poetic help from the force which perpetuates the species, figured as the goddess of erotic love.'[1]

3. Venus was a thoroughly Roman goddess. As Vergil took the legend that her son, the Trojan Aeneas, settled in Italy and was the ancestor of Romulus, as the basis of his great epic of Rome, so Lucretius here speaks as a patriotic Roman.

The reader will find some truth in all three views, no doubt, especially the second. Meanwhile, we cannot acquit Lucretius of inconsistency, but why should we? A Soviet leader publicly invoked the name of God in a recent speech, and the story is told of an eager young Russian girl, who had just taken an important examination in Marxism, rushing home to check her answers. There was one, in particular, she was not at all sure of. The question had been: 'What inscription concerning religion is written on one of Moscow's main gates?' After much head-scratching she had written her answer: 'Religion is the opiate of the masses.' Feverishly she looked it up in her textbook and found she was right. In profound relief she thereupon knelt down and thanked God. Mankind, we may say, paraphrasing T. S. Eliot, cannot bear very much consistency. *+ Mars section following v. imported.*

✓ [2. Exhortation to the Reader: the Origin of Matter]

(I. 50–61)

Lucretius now, as in most of the poem, addresses the reader in the person of his patron Memmius,[2] and explains the theme of his poem:

---

[1] *Black Ship to Hell*, p. 198.   [2] See Introduction, p. xii.

'Now turn your mind to philosophy. I propose to expound (i) heaven and the gods, (ii) the elements of matter.'

This short paragraph leads to Lucretius' eulogy of Epicurus as the first man to defy religion and teach the true Laws of Nature (extract no. 3). From this he passes to his own powerful condemnation of 'religion', whose evils are shown in such unholy deeds as the sacrifice of Iphigenia by her own father Agamemnon (extract no. 4).

Quod superest, vacuas auris animumque sagacem   50
semotum a curis adhibe veram ad rationem,
ne mea dona tibi studio disposta fideli,
intellecta prius quam sint, contempta relinquas.
nam tibi de summa caeli ratione deumque
disserere incipiam et rerum primordia pandam,   55
unde omnis natura creet res auctet alatque
quove eadem rursum natura perempta resolvat,
quae nos materiem et genitalia corpora rebus
reddunda in ratione vocare et semina rerum
appellare suëmus et haec eadem usurpare   60
corpora prima, quod ex illis sunt omnia primis.

The prosaic style of this paragraph contrasts strangely with the artistry and fluency of the following passages. Lucretius is an uneven poet—like Wordsworth, who could write not only such sublime lines as

> It is a beauteous evening, calm and free;
> The holy time is quiet as a nun,
> Breathless with adoration . . .

but also

> I've measured it from side to side;
> 'Tis three feet long, and two feet wide.

It is nevertheless of great interest because it clearly indicates a division of the book's subject-matter along two principal lines: first, the nature of the gods, and second, the nature of physical reality. This second theme occupies most of Lucretius' attention in Book I, so possibly he intended a separate book on the first. However that may be, by putting gods and atoms side by side here, he does show that the real subject of his poem is the opposition between science and religion.

3. Religion Overthrown by Philosophy

(I. 62–79)

'When human life was cowering beneath religion, Epicurus first dared to lift his eyes and break through the barriers of nature. Victorious, he proclaimed the fixed limit to the powers of all things. Religion has been subdued; philosophy is triumphant.'

This paragraph might equally well be entitled 'Eulogy of Epicurus', for Lucretius has every intention of following his master's teaching. Clearly the Epicurean philosophy, having replaced 'religion' for its followers, did excite in them something akin to religious devotion: indeed Lucretius' attitude to Epicurus and his writings resembles that of a devout Communist to Marx and his.

Humana ante oculos foede cum vita iaceret
in terris oppressa gravi sub religione
quae caput a caeli regionibus ostendebat
horribili super aspectu mortalibus instans,   65
primum Graius homo mortalis tollere contra
est oculos ausus primusque obsistere contra,
quem neque fama deum nec fulmina nec minitanti
murmure compressit caelum, sed eo magis acrem
irritat animi virtutem, effringere ut arta   70
naturae primus portarum claustra cupiret.
ergo vivida vis animi pervicit, et extra
processit longe flammantia moenia mundi
atque omne immensum peragravit mente animoque,
unde refert nobis victor quid possit oriri,   75

quid nequeat, finita potestas denique cuique
quanam sit ratione atque alte terminus haerens.
quare religio pedibus subiecta vicissim
obteritur, nos exaequat victoria caelo.

There is no doubt that 'religion' was the enemy for Lucretius.
But so it was for the Hebrew prophets: e.g. 'I hate, I despise your
feasts, and I will take no delight in your solemn assemblies.'[1] 'To
what purpose is the multitude of your sacrifices unto me? saith the
Lord.'[2] It may be said that they, unlike Lucretius, did not contemplate the disappearance of religion;[3] yet they were as much
against the debased religion of their time as Lucretius was against
that of his. Does not his indignation suggest a sensitivity of spirit
which might itself be called religious? Indeed Cyril Bailey[4] has
maintained that Lucretius and Epicurus, though abominating
traditional religion, *did* leave room for a positive religion in the
sense of a right relationship between men and the divine. Three
points are made in evidence:

1. 'The knowledge that he has nothing to fear from the gods
   enables the Epicurean to contemplate the world with un-
   troubled mind, which is itself an act of worship.'
2. The Epicurean is committed to the imitation of the tranquil
   life of the gods, and it is promised that he will 'lead a life
   worthy of the gods'.[5]
3. Both Epicurus and Lucretius[6] speak of men receiving visions
   of the gods in language which suggests communion between
   gods and men.

If this is so, the strictures of Lucretius against debased religion
are rightly called 'prophetic'.

[1] Amos v. 21.
[2] Isaiah i. 11.
[3] Though John MacMurray has affirmed that 'the great contribution
of the Hebrew to religion was that he did away with it'.
[4] Commentary, Vol. I, p. 71.
[5] *dignam dis degere vitam*, III. 322.
[6] E.g. VI. 68–78.

4. Iphigenia at Aulis

(I. 80–101)

'I fear you may think my inquiry impious. On the contrary religion is the cause of impious actions, as when at Aulis Iphigenia was sacrificed to win a prosperous voyage for the Greek fleet. To such lengths can religion go.'

Iphigenia was the first-born and most beautiful daughter of Agamemnon and Clytemnestra. Agamemnon had once killed a stag in the grove of Artemis, and for that offence the goddess sent a calm which prevented the Greek fleet from leaving the port of Aulis, where it was assembled in readiness to sail against Troy. The seer Calchas declared that the only way to propitiate Artemis was to sacrifice Iphigenia. She was accordingly prevailed upon to make the journey to Aulis under the promise of being married to Achilles, and Clytemnestra accompanied her daughter thither for the 'wedding'.

According to the common tradition Iphigenia was indeed slain upon the altar. Lucretius follows this tradition, as does Tennyson in *A Dream of Fair Women:*

> The high masts flicker'd as they lay afloat;
> The crowds, the temples, waver'd, and the shore;
> The bright death quiver'd at the victim's throat;
> Touch'd; and I knew no more.

A wall-painting at Pompeii shows Odysseus and Diomedes lifting up Iphigenia in their arms and carrying her to the altar for sacrifice; Agamemnon turns away and covers his face, while Iphigenia stretches out her arms in prayer to the goddess.

The Athenian dramatist Euripides however, in his *Iphigenia at Aulis*, makes Iphigenia accept the sacrifice of her life for the good of Hellas and walk of her own accord to the altar. But, as the sacrificial knife falls, Iphigenia vanishes, and in her place a hind is seen dying. Calchas declares that Artemis has taken pity on the girl and wafted her to the gods.

Illud in his rebus vereor, ne forte rearis 80
impia te rationis inire elementa viamque
indugredi sceleris.   quod contra saepius illa
religio peperit scelerosa atque impia facta.
Aulide quo pacto Triviai virginis aram
Iphianassai turparunt sanguine foede 85
ductores Danaum delecti, prima virorum.
cui simul infula virgineos circumdata comptus
ex utraque pari malarum parte profusast,
et maestum simul ante aras adstare parentem
sensit et hunc propter ferrum celare ministros 90
aspectuque suo lacrimas effundere civis,
muta metu terram genibus summissa petebat.
nec miserae prodesse in tali tempore quibat
quod patrio princeps donarat nomine regem.
nam sublata virum manibus tremibundaque ad aras 95
deductast, non ut sollemni more sacrorum
perfecto posset claro comitari Hymenaeo,
sed casta inceste nubendi tempore in ipso
hostia concideret mactatu maesta parentis,
exitus ut classi felix faustusque daretur. 100
tantum religio potuit suadere malorum.

A passionate intensity breathes through these lines as they
proceed to their climax in the much-quoted denunciation of
'religion': *tantum religio potuit suadere malorum.* As already
stated, it is doubtful whether in Lucretius' own day genuine belief
in the Olympians still survived on a scale to merit such an attack;
but whatever its effect may have been on his contemporaries, we
do know that the reading of Lucretius was one of the factors in
Shelley's conversion to atheism while still at school. Nor is it
surprising that the passage so impressed another poet, for it is
composed with a consummate artistry which justifies Cicero's

description of the *De Rerum Natura* as *multae artis*.[1] This is particularly true of lines 95–100, in which the pathos of Iphigenia's position is enhanced by the powerful use of ambiguity: e.g. *sublata* (95) suggests the ceremony at a Roman wedding of forcibly taking the bride from her mother's arms, as well as the violent snatching of the sacrificial victim; *tremibunda* describes the terrified trembling of the victim and the pleasurable agitation of the bride; *deducta* (96) is regularly used of the sacrificial animal led to the slaughter and of the bride escorted from her father's house to her husband. Shakespeare makes similar use of ambiguity: e.g. Othello, when about to put out the candle and strangle his wife Desdemona as she lies asleep, soliloquizes: 'Put out the light, and then—put out the light.'

5. 'Nothing can be Created out of Nothing'

(I. 146–66)

'The darkness of mind which religion inflicts can be dispelled only by the knowledge of Nature, the first principle of which is: "Nothing is created out of nothing by divine power".'

Of knowledge in general we know that Epicurus held an extremely low opinion. He condemned, for example, poetry, music, and mathematics, because they never made anyone happier, and despised technical logic and dialectic. He was, in fact, more contemptuous of learning and culture than any other philosopher has ever been. But the one study in which he was willing to engage was the study of Nature, because by it the superstitious fears which spring from belief in gods could be for ever banished. For, once the true causes of things were discovered, it would be seen that the gods, though they exist, have nothing whatever to do with anything that happens. Everything happens by natural, as opposed to supernatural, causes. This is the basis of Epicurean metaphysics.

[1] See Introduction p. xii.

Hunc igitur terrorem animi tenebrasque necessest
non radii solis neque lucida tela diei
discutiant, sed naturae species ratioque.
principium cuius hinc nobis exordia sumet,
nullam rem e nilo gigni divinitus umquam.   150
quippe ita formido mortalis continet omnis,
quod multa in terris fieri caeloque tuentur
quorum operum causas nulla ratione videre
possunt ac fieri divino numine rentur.
quas ob res ubi viderimus nil posse creari   155
de nilo, tum quod sequimur iam rectius inde
perspiciemus, et unde queat res quaeque creari
et quo quaeque modo fiant opera sine divum.
nam si de nilo fierent, ex omnibu' rebus
omne genus nasci posset, nil semine egeret.   160
e mare primum homines, e terra posset oriri
squamigerum genus et volucres erumpere caelo;
armenta atque aliae pecudes, genus omne ferarum,
incerto partu culta ac deserta tenerent.
nec fructus idem arboribus constare solerent,   165
sed mutarentur, ferre omnes omnia possent.

That 'nothing comes from nothing' was a belief common to all the Greek physical philosophers, according to Aristotle. Significantly Lucretius adds *divinitus* (150) and again *divino numine* (154), because 'religion', he asserts, is the source of mental darkness.

It is interesting to notice that the Christian philosophers of the first four centuries A.D. consistently maintained that God did create the universe *ex nihilo*: e.g. Irenaeus (end of the second century) asserted: 'While men cannot make anything out of nothing, but only out of matter already existing, yet God is in this point pre-eminently superior to men, that He Himself called into being the substance of His creation, when previously it had no existence.'[1]

They refused to accept what seems the common-sense view that *ex nihilo nihil fit*, as applied to Creation, because they believed that, if the created universe were conceived of as apart from God, the human mind would be driven to resolve this dualism either by denying the existence of the universe (as in some Eastern religions), or by denying the existence of God (which Epicurean philosophy, if consistent, would assuredly have done).

Strangely enough in our own day some support is given to the idea of creation *ex nihilo* by the 'steady state' or 'continuous creation' theory of Hoyle and Bondi, which asserts that new matter is constantly being created out of nothing to replenish the ever-expanding universe:

'New material is constantly being created so as to maintain a constant density in the background material. Where does this continually created material come from? Matter simply appears. It is created.'[2]

It is just to point out that this theory is opposed by Professor Ryle of Cambridge and many others, and also that Hoyle himself has since stated that his theory may need considerable modification in the light of further recent discoveries.

The argument in lines 159–66 is: *nothing can arise from nothing, for otherwise anything can arise from anything*. This does not follow as a matter of inevitable logic. But what Lucretius intends is not so much a formal proof of the proposition *nothing can come from nothing* as an extended illustration of what he means by it. Our observation of Nature, he argues, should convince us that we live in a *uni*verse, not a *multi*verse; everywhere we see that causes produce appropriate effects; therefore it makes better sense of our observation and experience to conclude that all things are produced from the fixed units of matter—the atoms—than that they 'just happen'.

This argument from the regularity of Nature impressed New-

---

[1] *Adversus Haereses*, II. 10. 3.
[2] Hoyle, *The Nature of the Universe*, p. 104.

ton, who was himself a convinced 'atomist'. The atom has been
shattered, but not Lucretius' desire for rational conclusions based
on evidence, nor his delight in seeking to understand the working
of the universe: and these two qualities are among the most
valuable, if not the most spectacular, benefits of the scientific
outlook.

6. The Invisibility of Atoms

(I. 265–89)

'All things are composed of invisible particles—atoms. You may
doubt the existence of such particles because they are unseen.
But consider other things which, though unseen, indicate their
existence by their effects, e.g. the wind, which, when stirred up,
sweeps sea, sky, and land with devastating effect.'

Nunc age, res quoniam docui non posse creari   265
de nilo neque item genitas ad nil revocari,
ne qua forte tamen coeptes diffidere dictis,
quod nequeunt oculis rerum primordia cerni,
accipe praeterea quae corpora tute necessest
confiteare esse in rebus nec posse videri.   270
principio venti vis verberat incita pontum
ingentisque ruit navis et nubila differt,
interdum rapido percurrens turbine campos
arboribus magnis sternit montisque supremos
silvifragis vexat flabris: ita perfurit acri   275
cum fremitu saevitque minaci murmure ventus.
sunt igitur venti nimirum corpora caeca
quae mare, quae terras, quae denique nubila caeli
verrunt ac subito vexantia turbine raptant,
nec ratione fluunt alia stragemque propagant   280
et cum mollis aquae fertur natura repente ——— →

flumine abundanti, quam largis imbribus auget
montibus ex altis magnus decursus aquai,
fragmina coniciens silvarum arbustaque tota,
nec validi possunt pontes venientis aquai ——> 285
vim subitam tolerare: ita magno turbidus imbri —— >
molibus incurrit validis cum viribus amnis.
dat sonitu magno stragem volvitque sub undis
grandia saxa ruitque et quidquid fluctibus obstat.

These lines expose a weakness in the Epicurean system, which it shares with some other 'common-sense' philosophies. While claiming to demand no more than trust in the evidence of the senses as its primary criterion of truth, it in fact postulated as the basis of reality invisible atoms. Since their existence could not be perceived through any of the senses, and in the absence of scientific instruments and highly developed powers of measurement such as we possess, Epicurus, and Lucretius after him, had to fall back on the argument from analogy, as here. But an analogy, however striking, can never be a proof.

Epicurus and Lucretius might have drawn comfort from the fact that scientists did not scorn the use of pictorial analogies in working on atomic theory till quite recently. Dalton, the father of nineteenth-century physics, 'pictured' the atom as a hard, concrete entity like a billiard ball. Rutherford and Bohr, in working out a new theory of the atom's structure at the beginning of this century, pictured it rather as a minute solar system, with a central nucleus and a number of electrons 'in orbit' around it. But in the 1920's Planck and Schroedinger pointed out that the atom cannot be pictured. Certainly present scientific theories of the atom are of a complex mathematical nature far removed from pictures.

After five lines of abstract theory Lucretius spends twenty-four on concrete illustration, to show how argument concerning things unseen must be by inference from what is seen. Epicurus had been content to make the abstract point alone, as he was a philosopher thinking out a rational system. But Lucretius was a poet as well as a thinker, and primarily a poet, seeing things not only as abstractions, but in vivid pictures. There have been those with the poet's vision, but with nothing particular to teach: with them the picture is all. Lucretius stands at the opposite extreme: his description is powerfully vivid, but springs directly from his desire to communicate thought—to teach, in fact.

7. The Poem's Purpose

(I. 921–50)

After a long discussion of rival philosophies, Lucretius returns to the exposition of the atomic system. But he pauses first to address a vivid and powerful exhortation to the reader similar to that at the beginning of the book:

'The hope of fame spurs me on. I am treading new ground for a poet. My purpose is to free men's minds from superstition, and I am adorning obscure thoughts with the beauty of poetry, as physicians deceive children into drinking bitter medicine by smearing honey on the lip of the cup. So my theme may seem tedious, but I am touching it with the honey of the Muses to hold your attention.'

Once more Lucretius insists that his aim in composing the poem is to overcome men's bondage to superstition by revealing the truth about the universe and human life. The only remedy for false 'religion' is true philosophy, and to its exposition he devotes all his art.

Nunc age quod superest cognosce et clarius audi.
nec me animi fallit quam sint obscura; sed acri
percussit thyrso laudis spes magna meum cor
et simul incussit suavem mi in pectus amorem
musarum, quo nunc instinctus mente vigenti   925
avia Pieridum peragro loca nullius ante
trita solo.   iuvat integros accedere fontis
atque haurire, iuvatque novos decerpere flores

insignemque meo capiti petere inde coronam
unde prius nulli velarint tempora musae;   930
primum quod magnis doceo de rebus et artis
religionum animum nodis exsolvere pergo,
deinde quod obscura de re tam lucida pango
carmina, musaeo contingens cuncta lepore.
id quoque enim non ab nulla ratione videtur;   935
sed veluti pueris absinthia taetra medentes
cum dare conantur, prius oras pocula circum
contingunt mellis dulci flavoque liquore,
ut puerorum aetas improvida ludificetur
labrorum tenus, interea perpotet amarum   940
absinthi laticem deceptaque non capiatur,
sed potius tali pacto recreata valescat;
sic ego nunc, quoniam haec ratio plerumque videtur
tristior esse quibus non est tractata, retroque
vulgus abhorret ab hac, volui tibi suaviloquenti   945
carmine Pierio rationem exponere nostram
et quasi musaeo dulci contingere melle,
si tibi forte animum tali ratione tenere
versibus in nostris possem, dum perspicis omnem
naturam rerum qua constet compta figura.   950

My art is not without a purpose.[1] Lucretius stands at the opposite extreme from those who believe in 'art for art's sake' and practise 'style'. For Lucretius the truth of his doctrine was all-important, and style was simply the most energetic and attractive way he could find to expound that truth. How he would have despised Walter Pater, and how much he would have applauded George Bernard Shaw! The latter wrote, in the Preface to *Man and Superman*:

'No doubt I must recognize, as even the Ancient Mariner did,

---

[1] R. E. Latham's rendering of line 935.

that I must tell my story entertainingly if I am to hold the wedding guest spellbound in spite of the siren sounds of the loud bassoon. But "for art's sake" alone I would not face the toil of writing a single sentence. I know that there are men who, having nothing to say and nothing to write, are nevertheless so in love with oratory and with literature that they delight in repeating as much as they can understand of what others have said or written aforetime. . . . But a true original style is never achieved for its own sake. . . . He who has nothing to assert has no style and can have none: he who has something to assert will go as far in power of style as its momentousness and his conviction will carry him.'

Lucretius, like Shaw, 'refutes the parrot cry that art should never be didactic'.[1] For him too 'great art can never be anything else'.[1]

[1] Preface to *Pygmalion*.

BOOK II

IT is only by discovering the truth about the universe that man can be set free from the bondage and degradation of religion, Lucretius asserts; only so also can he be set free for living the good life. Since only physical science, as revealed in the Epicurean system, can provide that truth, Lucretius now proceeds to explore Epicurean physics in detail. He deals carefully with such matters as the shape and size of atoms, all in verse which never flags and often soars to surprising vividness and beauty.

We have mentioned the good life, and it is just the linking of ethics with physics which makes this book of living interest. In extract no. 8 we have Lucretius' most explicit description of the Epicurean philosophy as a way of life. Most philosophers have been concerned not only to interpret the universe, but also to ask questions about human life. What is the supreme end of human existence? Is it training for some sort of perfection, as Plato and many Christian philosophers have held? Or is it devotion to duty, that 'stern daughter of the voice of God', as the Stoics in the ancient world and Immanuel Kant in the modern age believed? It was neither of these, Epicurus declared, but pleasure. He went on to make it clear that he did not mean such gross and unrestrained pleasures as Aristippus and the Cyrenaic philosophers had recommended, for these would only bring pain as an inevitable consequence. The wise man, he taught, must aim at a state of equilibrium, in which refined bodily pleasure might be secured by the simple life, and the pains which attacked the body relieved, as far as possible, by simple treatment. Meanwhile, and more importantly, the mind must be released from its own characteristic pains, such as ambition, anxiety, and the superstitious dread of the gods, by a philosophy which could lay bare the true nature of reality.

Epicurus sought to build a wall of 'self-sufficiency and serenity' (αὐτάρκεια καὶ ἀταραξία), within which the enlightened human spirit could develop, secure from the changes and chances of the outside world, where violence, greed, and crude superstition seemed to rule. So he withdrew from the troubled political and social scene of his own day, and lived with his disciples in his quiet Athenian garden, avoiding the world of politics and ambition, leading a simple life of unassuming and undemanding happiness, enjoying what Tennyson called

> the sober majesties
> Of settled, sweet, Epicurean life.[1]

And he would certainly have applauded Tennyson's other lines:

> Stately purpose, valour in battle, glorious annals of army and fleet,
> Death for the right cause, death for the wrong cause, trumpets of victory, groans of defeat;
> Raving politics never at rest—as this poor earth's history runs,
> What is it all but a trouble of ants in the gleam of a million suns?[2]

That this amiable, though egoistic creed can still exert an appeal, has been shown by the growth of the 'Beatnik' movement in America during the last decade. Two of its prominent exponents defined their movement in the following thoroughly Epicurean terms: 'The "Beat" is that generation which has turned its back on the eternal rat-race, desiring not to change the world, but rather to deaden the pain of having to live in it.'[3] It would seem from this that, for some, the Epicurean ethic is very up to date.

Needless to say, the same cannot be asserted of Epicurean physics, which has been rendered completely obsolete by the exciting scientific discoveries of our own century. What then has happened to the 'indestructible' atom on whose shape and movements Lucretius lavishes such attention in his book, and which was accepted so whole-heartedly by nineteenth-century science? It was John Dalton (1766–1844) who took over the atomic hypothesis: investigation and experiment seemed to confirm the pic-

---

[1] *Lucretius*, ll. 217–18. [2] *Vastness*, II, IV.
[3] Feldman and Gartenberg, *Protest*, p. 21.

ture of the physical universe as reducible to minute, hard, billiard-ball-like entities. But at the end of that century Sir J. J. Thomson (1856–1940) discovered the electron. In this century Rutherford and Bohr worked out a new picture of the atom—as a minute solar system, consisting of a central nucleus which carried a positive electrical charge, round which electrons, each carrying a negative charge, rotated in orbit. Subsequent researches have greatly modified this conception, especially Einstein's discovery of the relation between energy and mass. The 'solar system' view of the atom has been replaced by the conception of matter as consisting of fields of energy which are related in a complex way only describable by mathematical symbols.

At the same time the relativity physics of Einstein has altered the rigid determinism associated with the Newtonian view. Space and time are no longer absolutes, as they were for him. Substance is not something extended in space and persistent in time, but rather a series of events which take place in space-time. Further, Planck and Bohr, in the early years of this century, showed that changes within the atomic structure happen by sudden 'jumps'. Heisenberg proceeded from this to postulate his Principle of Uncertainty, which shows that we cannot at the same time determine accurately both the position and the velocity of a particular sub-atomic particle. When we try to observe what goes on within the minute world of the atom, the very tools used in observation disturb the relationships of that world. The law of cause and effect *may* run there, but it cannot be observed and measured with complete accuracy, and it therefore becomes a philosophic rather than a scientific concept. 'It is as though we had tracked the cause-and-effect relationship down through natural phenomena of all sorts, and when arriving at its ultimate lair, the ultimate particles, we had found the door bolted from the inside.'[1]

We may be sure that scientists will continue to search for ways of opening the door. They will do so by making hypotheses about the ultimate nature of reality, as the early Greek atomists, followed by Epicurus and Lucretius, did. But they will differ from them profoundly in two important ways. They will, certainly,

[1] S. Beck, *The Simplicity of Science*, p. 130.

test all hypotheses by the most detailed and stringent techniques that an increasingly sophisticated mathematics can supply. And they will not, we hope, make the mistake of Epicurus and many other thinkers of imagining that they have discovered the final, complete explanation of reality. For, with the advantage of hindsight, they will know that the history of human thought in all its branches, including scientific thought, is littered with discarded 'final truths'. It is conceivable that, twenty centuries from now, our 'modern' science will be as dated as that of Epicurus and Lucretius. Nevertheless, we hope that the writings of such scientists as Einstein will still be read for the beauty and lucidity of their thought. It is for the same reason that we commend the following extracts to the reader.

8. The Blessedness of Epicurean Philosophy

(II. 1–33)

'It is a pleasure to watch from the safety of land the perils of storm-bound voyagers, or to behold a military battle without being involved. But the greatest pleasure is to look down, from the pinnacle of philosophy, on the errors and follies of mankind, struggling for wealth and power. Men are blind not to see that human nature requires for true happiness only freedom from pain for the body and for the mind freedom from fear.'

Following the text is Calverley's rendering of the passage, remarkable for its vigorous English hexameters, as well as for its line-by-line correspondence to the Latin.

Suave, mari magno turbantibus aequora ventis,
e terra magnum alterius spectare laborem;
non quia vexari quemquamst iucunda voluptas,
sed quibus ipse malis careas quia cernere suave est.
suave etiam belli certamina magna tueri   5
per campos instructa tua sine parte pericli.

sed nil dulcius est, bene quam munita tenere
edita doctrina sapientum templa serena,
despicere unde queas alios passimque videre
errare atque viam palantis quaerere vitae,   10
certare ingenio, contendere nobilitate,
noctes atque dies niti praestante labore
ad summas emergere opes rerumque potiri.
o miseras hominum mentis, o pectora caeca!
qualibus in tenebris vitae quantisque periclis   15
degitur hoc aevi quodcumquest! nonne videre
nil aliud sibi naturam latrare, nisi utqui
corpore seiunctus dolor absit, mente fruatur
iucundo sensu cura semota metuque?
ergo corpoream ad naturam pauca videmus   20
esse opus omnino, quae demant cumque dolorem,
delicias quoque uti multas substernere possint;
gratius interdum neque natura ipsa requirit,
si non aurea sunt iuvenum simulacra per aedes
lampadas igniferas manibus retinentia dextris,   25
lumina nocturnis epulis ut suppeditentur,
nec domus argento fulget auroque renidet
nec citharae reboant laqueata aurataque templa,
cum tamen inter se prostrati in gramine molli
propter aquae rivum sub ramis arboris altae   30
non magnis opibus iucunde corpora curant,
praesertim cum tempestas arridet et anni
tempora conspergunt viridantis floribus herbas.

Sweet, when the great sea's water is stirred to his depths by the
    storm-winds,
Standing ashore to descry one afar-off mightily struggling:
Not that a neighbour's sorrow to you yields dulcet enjoyment:

But that the sight hath a sweetness, of ills ourselves are exempt
    from.
Sweet too 'tis to behold, on a broad plain mustering, war hosts
Arm them for some great battle, one's self unscathed by the
    danger:—
Yet still happier this: to possess, impregnably guarded,
Those calm heights of the sages, which have for an origin
    Wisdom:
Thence to survey our fellows, observe them this way and that way
Wander amidst Life's path, poor stragglers seeking a highway:
Watch mind battle with mind, and escutcheon rival escutcheon:
Gaze on that untold strife, which is waged 'neath the sun and the
    starlight,
Up as they toil on the surface whereon rest Riches and Empire.
O race born unto trouble! O minds all lacking of eyesight!
'Neath what a vital darkness, amidst how terrible dangers
Move ye thro' this thing Life, this fragment! Fools that ye hear
    not
Nature clamour aloud for the one thing only: that, all pain
Parted and passed from the body, the mind too bask in a blissful
Dream, all fear of the future and all anxiety over!
Now as regards man's body, a few things only are needful,
(Few, tho' we sum up all), to remove all misery from him,
Aye, and to strew in his path such a lib'ral carpet of pleasures
That scarce Nature herself would at times ask happiness greater.
Statues of youth and of beauty may not gleam golden around him,
(Each in his right hand bearing a great lamp lustrously burning,
Whence to the midnight revel a light may be furnished always),
Silver may not shine softly, nor gold blaze bright, in his mansion,
Nor to the noise of the tabret his halls gold-cornicëd echo:—
Yet still he, with his fellow, reposed on the velvety greensward,
Near to a rippling stream, by a tall tree canopied over,
Shall, though they lack great riches, enjoy all bodily pleasure:
Chiefliest then when above them a fair sky smiles, and the young
    year
Flings with a bounteous hand over each green meadow the wild-
    flowers.

The German word *Schadenfreude* has in recent years been
borrowed to express the feeling of pleasure which arises from
observing, or knowing of, the misfortunes of others, portrayed
by Lucretius at the beginning of this passage, In less technical
language, the expression 'I'm all right, Jack!' has become common
currency to describe, and condemn, just this attitude of selfish
egoism. But three mitigating factors may be urged on Lucretius'
behalf:

1. The sentiment and the metaphor seem to have been a commonplace in both Greek and Latin literature. Munro quotes a fragment from Greek comedy: 'How sweet it is, mother, to behold the
sea from the land, when one is not sailing himself.'[1] Cicero also,
writing to Atticus, says: *nunc vero, cum cogar exire de navi, non
abiectis sed ereptis gubernaculis, cupio istorum naufragia ex terra
intueri.*[2]

2. Lucretius does soften this un-magnanimous sentiment in
lines 3 and 4. This is more than can be said for St. Thomas
Aquinas, the great theologian of the Medieval Church (and usually
described as the 'Angelic Doctor'), who wrote thus:

'Nothing should be denied to the blessed which belongs to the
perfection of their beatitude. . . . Wherefore, in order that the
happiness of the saints may be more delightful to them, . . . they
are permitted to see perfectly the suffering of the damned.'[3]

3. Both Lucretius and Epicurus—and, let us hope, Aquinas!
—were better than their creed at this point. We know that
Epicurus was a kindly, humane man, and Lucretius shows
throughout his poem that he is sensitive to human suffering. In
any case why does Lucretius seek so earnestly to convert his
readers to his creed, if he is unconcerned with their condition?

9. The Dance of the Atoms
(II. 80–99)

'Atoms are ceaselessly moving in the infinite void, either by their
own inherent motion or through collision with other atoms.'

[1] Archippus (Kock, fr. 43).   [2] *ad Att.* II. 7. 4.
[3] *Summa Theologiae* III, Question 94.

From ethics Lucretius turns resolutely to physics, for Epicurus had said: 'Without natural science we cannot enjoy unmixed pleasure.'[1] The supreme end of life is pleasure, but this can only be achieved through knowing how the universe is constituted. Knowledge of reality sets men free from the dream-world of superstition, and shows them how to live.

Epicurean physics asserts that the universe contains atoms and 'void' (*inane* 83), i.e. empty space: all matter is made up of a mixture of the two in various proportions. This was also a cardinal tenet of the 'atomic' philosophers, Leucippus and Democritus. In this they sharply differed from their predecessors, the Eleatics, whose founder Parmenides stubbornly affirmed that the universe was one solid, motionless, changeless mass, and that separate objects and motion were a delusion, for 'that which is not does not exist'. Leucippus overcame this seemingly invincible proposition by postulating that 'that which is not does exist', in the sense of non-corporeal existence—empty space.

With this part of the atomic philosophy Epicurus thoroughly agreed. And the main argument he adduced for the existence of void was that without it there could be no motion, and therefore the existence of compound bodies would be impossible: 'the atoms move continuously throughout eternity', he states.[2] Democritus seems to have held that, while 'free' atoms were always moving in all directions, once they formed compounds they were interlocked and adopted the motion of the whole compound body, just as the passenger in a vehicle inevitably adopts its motion. By contrast, Epicurus was concerned to show that atoms never rest, or lose their original motion, but move eternally from one collision to another. Even in a compound the constituent atoms, though forming a harmony, are in constant motion in all directions.

Si cessare putas rerum primordia posse   80
cessandoque novos rerum progignere motus,
avius a vera longe ratione vagaris.

[1] Diogenes Laertius X. 143 (see Introduction, p. xiv).
[2] *Ep. ad Hdt.* 43.

nam quoniam per inane vagantur, cuncta necessest
aut gravitate sua ferri primordia rerum
aut ictu forte alterius.   nam cum cita saepe   85
obvia conflixere, fit ut diversa repente
dissiliant; neque enim mirum, durissima quae sint
ponderibus solidis neque quicquam a tergo ibus obstet.
et quo iactari magis omnia materiai
corpora pervideas, reminiscere totius imum   90
nil esse in summa, neque habere ubi corpora prima
consistant, quoniam spatium sine fine modoquest,
immensumque patere in cunctas undique partis,
pluribus ostendi et certa ratione probatumst.
quod quoniam constat, nimirum nulla quies est   95
reddita corporibus primis per inane profundum,
sed magis assiduo varioque exercita motu
partim intervallis magnis confulta resultant,
pars etiam brevibus spatiis vexantur ab ictu.

Atoms move in different directions because space is infinite,
says Lucretius (89–94): if it were finite, they would all end up at
the bottom. Is space infinite? Most modern physicists would
regard this question as unanswerable, since we have no suitable
means of measurement. Hoyle's new geometry of the universe may
make the problem clearer—always provided that we can understand the complicated mathematics on which it is based. Meanwhile some cosmologists speak of space as finite and boundless,
and suggest the following analogy. Imagine a two-dimensional
creature confined to the surface of a sphere: for him that sphere
would be limitless. So, a three-dimensional being like man may
find a four-dimensional universe finite yet boundless.

10. An Illustration of Atomic Movement

(II. 112–41)

'The movement of motes in a sunbeam provides a picture of the movement of atoms and is an actual outcome of atomic movement. For the single atoms unite into small compounds, as yet invisible, then form larger bodies which are seen to move in the sun.'

This passage is an excellent example of Lucretius' power to combine imaginative richness with technical clarity. The illustration itself is not original, however, and may even have been a commonplace among the atomists. Lactantius, writing of Leucippus, says: *haec, inquit, per inane irrequietis motibus volitant et huc atque illuc feruntur, sicut pulveris minutias videmus in sole, cum per fenestram radios ac lumen immiserit.*[1]

Cuius, uti memoro, rei simulacrum et imago
ante oculos semper nobis versatur et instat.
contemplator enim, cum solis lumina cumque
inserti fundunt radii per opaca domorum: 115
multa minuta modis multis per inane videbis
corpora misceri radiorum lumine in ipso
et velut aeterno certamine proelia pugnas
edere turmatim certantia nec dare pausam,
conciliis et discidiis exercita crebris;   120
conicere ut possis ex hoc, primordia rerum
quale sit in magno iactari semper inani.
dumtaxat rerum magnarum parva potest res
exemplare dare et vestigia notitiai.
hoc etiam magis haec animum te advertere par est   125
corpora quae in solis radiis turbare videntur,
quod tales turbae motus quoque materiai
significant clandestinos caecosque subesse.

[1] *De Ira Dei*, 10. 9.

multa videbis enim plagis ibi percita caecis
commutare viam retroque repulsa reverti 130
nunc huc nunc illuc in cunctas undique partis
scilicet hic a principiis est omnibus error.
prima moventur enim per se primordia rerum;
inde ea quae parvo sunt corpora conciliatu
et quasi proxima sunt ad viris principiorum, 135
ictibus illorum caecis impulsa cientur,
ipsaque proporro paulo maiora lacessunt.
sic a principiis ascendit motus et exit
paulatim nostros ad sensus, ut moveantur
illa quoque, in solis quae lumine cernere quimus 140
nec quibus id·faciant plagis apparet aperte.

11. The Swerve of the Atoms

(II. 216–24)

'The atoms, while travelling downward through space in parallel lines, swerve from the perpendicular by a minute amount, at quite undetermined times and places. Without this swerve there could have been no atomic collisions and hence no creation.'

Illud in his quoque te rebus cognoscere avemus,
corpora cum deorsum rectum per inane feruntur
ponderibus propriis, incerto tempore ferme
incertisque locis spatio depellere paulum,
tantum quod momen mutatum dicere possis. 220
quod nisi declinare solerent, omnia deorsum,
imbris uti guttae, caderent per inane profundum,
nec foret offensus natus nec plaga creata
principiis: ita nil umquam natura creasset.

The theory of the 'swerve'—in Greek *parenclisis* (παρέγκλισις), in Latin *declinatio* or *clinamen*—was important for Epicurean philosophy, both in its explanation of the physical universe and in its treatment of human behaviour. Here, as before, ethics and physics are linked together.

1. The swerve is important physically, as an explanation of the fundamental creative process. So far the picture presented has been of atoms falling at equal speeds downward in the void. They fall downward because of their weight, which is the fundamental cause of their motion. And they fall at equal speeds because the void, unlike a physical medium such as air or water, offers no resistance to their fall. So they might proceed, like an endless column of marching soldiers, never touching, always equidistant. In order that they may interact and form the compound objects which we see, there must be an occasional and unpredictable swerve, which, like one soldier in the column lurching or breaking step, upsets the orderly ranks of atoms and sets in train endless creative collisions.

2. The swerve is important ethically, for Epicureans believed in free will, unlike the atomists and the Stoics, who were determinists. It was clear to Epicurus that he must postulate free will as an exception to the general reign of law in the universe. Otherwise man would exchange one form of servitude for another: he would imagine himself under the irrational dominion of destiny instead of that of the gods. And Lucretius proceeds to argue (II. 251–88) from free will as a fact of everyday experience to the theory of occasional atomic irregularity.

The fact that modern physics has discovered just such 'irregularity' within the atom, has tempted some writers like Sir James Jeans to argue that this vindicates free will. Such a proceeding is as misguided as that of the Victorian scientists who rushed to a denial of free will because of the strict determinism of Newtonian physics. The fact that the behaviour of sub-atomic particles is unpredictable does not prove that they have no cause. Such phrases as 'the free will of the atom' are merely a misguided way of expressing our ignorance of what actually happens at this level of physical reality.

Incidentally, even if modern physics can be said to have modified its former strict determinism, we find a strange paradox when we consider the specific science of human behaviour. For in the two most important schools of psychology, the Freudian and the Behaviourist, determinism rules. Though radically opposed in almost everything else, they are united in holding at any rate in their unmodified forms a rigid determinism. In the Freudian system it is the Unconscious which controls and determines behaviour; in Behaviourism it is the physico-chemical reactions of the brain and nervous system. The fact that these schools are so bitterly opposed suggests that their theories may not be altogether acceptable in their unmodified form.

To sum up, we may say that the Epicurean 'swerve' was a daring and legitimate speculation in its time, though it was rendered obsolete as a physical theory by Newton's laws of motion (which have themselves been rendered obsolete in the sub-atomic world of modern physics). But the ethical theory of free-will to which the physical theory was attached is by no means obsolete. Against the many powerful arguments which would destroy the freedom of the will we have not yet found a better reply than Epicurus' common-sense assertion that freedom is a primary datum of the human consciousness. Whatever the rival disputants—who too often take up extreme positions—may say, the ordinary introspection of a sane man in more or less normal health does seem to indicate awareness of some degree of freedom, however limited. This, inevitably, makes the absolute predictability of human behaviour an unattainable goal, and constitutes a severe rebuff to some schools of psychology. But the psychologists may take comfort from modern physics, where absolute predictability, such as Laplace dreamed of, is already out of date, having been replaced, especially where cosmic and microcosmic scales of measurement are concerned, by statistical predictability.

Meanwhile, the 'swerve' suggests a further analogy between physics and ethics which the reader may wish to pursue. As we have already stated (p. 36): 'The fact that the behaviour of the sub-atomic particles is unpredictable does not prove that they have no cause.' Perhaps the same could be said of human behaviour, and Professor A. J. Ayer, in a lucid discussion of the subject entitled *Man as a Subject for Science* (The Auguste Comte Memorial Lecture for 1964), makes this point. He reaches the tentative conclusion that, though the antithesis between free will and determinism may be illusory, most people tenaciously hold the position that free will means that we are responsible for our actions, and determinism means that we are not. He concludes: 'Since it is not at all clear why one's responsibility for an action should depend on its being causally inexplicable, this may only prove that people are irrational, but there it is. I am indeed strongly inclined to think that our ordinary ideas of freedom and responsibility are very muddle-headed; but for what they are worth, they are also very firmly held. It would not be at all easy to estimate the social consequences of discarding them.'[1] It almost seems as though, if free will did not exist, it would be necessary to invent it.

12. The Variety of Atomic Shapes

(II. 333–70)

'Atoms are not all alike in shape, and there is an immense number of atoms for each shape. For, firstly, since atoms are infinite in number, they cannot be all of identical shape and form; secondly, individual members of the human race and that of the animals differ immensely, even within the species. Thus, when a calf is sacrificed, its distraught mother searches everywhere, and will not accept other calves as her own. So kids and lambs run to their own mothers for milk.'

Of the first argument we may simply say that it is a *non sequitur*. There is no reason at all why an infinite number of atoms should not be of the same shape and size. Argument two is an analogy (the weakest form of argument where strict proof is required) and not to be pressed. It does no more than point to the immense variety of all created things, and traces this back to a fundamental variety in the shape of the atoms. What will strike the reader most

[1] p. 26.

forcibly is not the argumentative, but the descriptive power of the
lines, the vivid and poignant picture of the cow seeking her lost
calf. Whatever Lucretius himself may have thought, this passage
shows that he was a poet first and a philosopher afterwards.

Nunc age iam deinceps cunctarum exordia rerum
qualia sint et quam longe distantia formis
percipe, multigenis quam sint variata figuris;   335
non quo multa parum simili sint praedita forma,
sed quia non vulgo paria omnibus omnia constant.
nec mirum; nam cum sit eorum copia tanta
ut neque finis, uti docui, neque summa sit ulla,
debent nimirum non omnibus omnia prorsum   340
esse pari filo similique adfecta figura.
praeterea genus humanum mutaeque natantes
squamigerum pecudes et laeta armenta feraeque
et variae volucres, laetantia quae loca aquarum
concelebrant circum ripas fontisque lacusque,   345
et quae pervulgant nemora avia pervolitantes;
quorum unum quidvis generatim sumere perge,
invenies tamen inter se differre figuris.
nec ratione alia proles cognoscere matrem
nec mater posset prolem; quod posse videmus   350
nec minus atque homines inter se nota cluere.
nam saepe ante deum vitulus delubra decora
turicremas propter mactatus concidit aras
sanguinis exspirans calidum de pectore flumen.
at mater viridis saltus orbata peragrans   355
quaerit humi pedibus vestigia pressa bisulcis,
omnia convisens oculis loca si queat usquam
conspicere amissum fetum, completque querellis
frondiferum nemus adsistens et crebra revisit

ad stabulum desiderio perfixa iuvenci,   360
nec tenerae salices atque herbae rore vigentes
fluminaque illa queunt summis labentia ripis
oblectare animum subitamque avertere curam,
nec vitulorum aliae species per pabula laeta
derivare queunt animum curaque levare: 365
usque adeo quiddam proprium notumque requirit.
praeterea teneri tremulis cum vocibus haedi
cornigeras norunt matres agnique petulci
balantum pecudes: ita, quod natura reposcit,
ad sua quisque fere decurrunt ubera lactis.   370

13. Nature's Variety Springs from Atomic Variety

(II. 581–99)

'It is the variety of atomic shapes which causes variety in things. The more powers and properties anything possesses, the greater the variety of atoms it must contain. Thus the earth contains the seeds of water, fire, crops, trees, rivers, pasture, and is therefore rightly called the "Universal Mother".'

The proposition here set out is linked to that of the last extract. Here, as there, it is the variety of visual products which points back to an original atomic variety. But here is introduced a variety of *qualities*, 'forces and powers', which are likewise held to stem from an original atomic variety. A compound consisting of atoms of only one class—so the argument runs—would have the least possible variety of combination and movement, and therefore the least possible amount of 'forces and powers'. On the other hand, a compound containing the largest number of classes of atoms— the earth itself—would have the greatest possible variety of powers.

Illud in his obsignatum quoque rebus habere
convenit et memori mandatum mente tenere,
nil esse, in promptu quorum natura videtur,
quod genere ex uno consistat principiorum,
nec quicquam quod non permixto semine constet;   585
et quodcumque magis vis multas possidet in se
atque potestates, ita plurima principiorum
in sese genera ac varias docet esse figuras.
principio tellus habet in se corpora prima
unde mare immensum volventes frigora fontes   590
assidue renovent, habet ignes unde oriantur.
nam multis succensa locis ardent sola terrae,
ex imis vero furit ignibus impetus Aetnae.
tum porro nitidas fruges arbustaque laeta
gentibus humanis habet unde extollere possit,   595
unde etiam fluvios frondis et pabula laeta
montivago generi possit praebere ferarum.
quare magna deum mater materque ferarum
et nostri genetrix haec dicta est corporis una.

The last six lines might be called a piece of Lucretian demythologizing, since he restates supernatural categories in terms consistent with scientific knowledge. He does not reject out of hand
the popular belief in the earth as Great Mother. Indeed, the belief
is seen to be valid, as expressing the recognition that mother earth
contains the seeds of all things, and she (not the gods) produces
fruit. But the personification of earth into a goddess is a superstitious delusion. This leads Lucretius to set out in detail (600–43)
a description of the Phrygian cult of Cybele, the Magna Mater,
which was brought to Rome and established as part of the State
religion more than a century before the time of Lucretius.

14. The Truth about the Gods and Nature

(II. 646–60)

'The gods have no concern with men, and the earth can be called "Mother of the Gods" only by allegory, since it is inanimate.'

From his description of the frenzied and orgiastic rites connected with the worship of the Great Mother, Lucretius now turns, by contrast, to the true life of the gods—serene, separate, untouched by any human activities, and with no concern for any human affairs. Then he rounds off his 'demythologizing' paragraphs by returning to the Earth Mother allegory. This is harmless, he says, so long as it is recognized as a piece of personification, but, if taken seriously, can lead to degrading superstition.

In the two lines immediately preceding this extract, Lucretius asserted that the Magna Mater cult is based on false beliefs: *enim* (646) introduces his reason for this assertion.

Omnis enim per se divum natura necessest
immortali aevo summa cum pace fruatur
semota ab nostris rebus seiunctaque longe.
nam privata dolore omni, privata periclis,
ipsa suis pollens opibus, nil indiga nostri,   650
nec bene promeritis capitur neque tangitur ira.
terra quidem vero caret omni tempore sensu,
et quia multarum potitur primordia rerum,
multa modis multis effert in lumina solis.
hic siquis mare Neptunum Cereremque vocare   655
constituet fruges et Bacchi nomine abuti
mavult quam laticis proprium proferre vocamen,
concedamus ut hic terrarum dictitet orbem
esse deum matrem, dum vera re tamen ipse
religione animum turpi contingere parcat.   660

This famous description of the life of the gods makes it clear that Lucretius, like Epicurus, has no doubt about the existence of divine beings. Epicurus[1] says: 'The gods exist, for our knowledge of them is clear. But they are not what the populace supposes them to be. . . . To destroy the gods of popular belief is not impiety; impiety is to ascribe to the gods what the populace believes of them. What is blessed and incorruptible neither troubles others nor is troubled itself, so that it feels neither anger towards us nor gratitude.' The gods, in fact, are models of that Epicurean serenity described in II. 1–33 (extract no. 8).

From the last six lines we gather what Lucretius regarded as the legitimate and illegitimate use of allegory. As a poet he had already used allegory in his opening invocation to Venus, 'the all-generating powers and genial heat of Nature'. He is also willing to follow popular usage on occasion and use the names of deities for their attributes.[2] But he may also be criticizing Stoic philosophers, who seem to have carried this kind of allegory to much greater lengths, and to have regarded the names of the gods as strictly personifications of parts of the universe, especially earth, sea, and sky.

In the last line the words *religione turpi* remind us of the real aim behind the many previous paragraphs devoted to the minute description of atomic behaviour. We need natural science, say Lucretius and Epicurus, to discover the truth about the universe, and hence to be finally set free from the falsity and degradation of popular religion.

[1] *Ep. ad Men.* 123.
[2] See commentary on extract no. 1, p. 10.

BOOK III

IN BOOK I Lucretius argued that we need science to discover the truth about the universe, for only so can we be freed from the untruths of religion, with its belief in capricious divine beings who constantly interfere in human affairs. In Book II he proceeded to work out the atomic system of Epicurus as a scientific account of reality. He also showed that the gods, so far from interfering with human beings, dwell apart and unconcerned. But almost as great a hindrance to the good life comes from man's superstitious fear of death. So in Book III Lucretius seeks to show how the Epicurean philosophy can enable us to face death unafraid, through the all-important knowledge that the soul is mortal. This vision of reality, with death ending all, so far from seeming cheerless and bleak to Lucretius, fills him with something akin to religious rapture. It comes to a climax in a 'Hymn' in praise of mortality—*nil igitur mors est ad nos neque pertinet hilum*[1] —which rivals in eloquence a poem of Dylan Thomas which could well provide a title for the whole book: 'And death shall have no dominion'.

But does not Lucretius protest too much about the dread of death and what comes after? Would not such contemporaries as read his work share the view of death given by Catullus in the famous love-poem *Vivamus, mea Lesbia, atque amemus*?[2] There the 'gather-ye-rosebuds-while-ye-may' sentiments of the first few lines are balanced by the chill and poignant reminder:

> *nobis cum semel occidit brevis lux,*
> *nox est perpetua una dormienda.*

Clearly Catullus believes that death ends all, and needs no philosophy to prove it. And Lucretius' other famous contemporary, Cicero, specifically criticizes Epicurus' statement that all men are terrified by stories of the after-life. Not even old women believe

---

[1] Line 830, extract no. 17.   [2] V.

them, he claims.[1] If this is so, it seems that Lucretius has exaggerated the rôle played by the fear of death, just as he did with the rôle played by religion in Book I, and that he has wrongly assumed the fear of punishment after death to be as prevalent in the Rome of his day as it was in the Athens of Epicurus' day.

On the other side it should be said that the Romans certainly took death seriously and were constantly aware of it. Even in Lucretius' day, death and burial were occasions for prolonged and complicated rites. Lamps and garlands would be strewn around the corpse, which was covered in wreaths. The women of the household repeated cries and lamentations at intervals, tearing their hair and beating their breasts. Though the funerals of the poor would be hurried and nocturnal, those of considerable people would be conducted with much pomp and publicity. Polybius, the Greek historian of the second century B.C., has left us an account of a Roman funeral which deeply moved him: 'An ambitious and virtuous young man could not easily see a nobler sight.'[2]

In the procession, each ancestor of the dead man was represented by a man in a mask, wearing the insignia of office which that ancestor had gained, as consul, praetor, etc. Others bore placards which recounted the achievements of the deceased. As the procession wound its way to the site of burial or cremation, women abandoned themselves to transports of grief. If the dead man had played any important part in public life, the procession would halt at the forum, while a son, close relative, or important official delivered a funeral oration. We are not to imagine this rising to the heights of M. Antony's speech over the body of Caesar. But the publicity which this and the rest of the burial customs gave to funerals must have made the average Roman far more conscious of death than we are. It is a commonplace that we, unlike our own Victorian ancestors, are increasingly frank about sex and reticent about death, which has replaced sex as the topic not to be mentioned among 'nice' people.[3]

[1] quaeve anus tam excors inveniri potest, quae ea quae quondam credebantur apud inferos portenta extimescat? (De Nat. Deorum I. 31.)   [2] Hist. VI. 2.
[3] See Geoffrey Gorer's Death, Grief and Mourning in Contemporary Britain.

We must add to this awareness of death the sheer weight of superstitious fear which seemed to be part of the atmosphere of Roman life, and from which not all sceptics would succeed in freeing themselves by conscious effort. If the younger Pliny a century later affirmed his belief in ghosts,[1] we may be sure that not all of Lucretius' contemporaries would be reassured by his rational explanation.[2] References abound to witches and vampires, and, after the flood of Graeco-Oriental superstition, to sorcerers and sorceresses with their sinister rites. If we add all this to the awareness of death, we may suspect that 'the fear of something after death' might well have a considerable hold upon ordinary men in Lucretius' day. And can we be sure that even philosophers would be proof against it in times of personal crisis? After all, that most rational of Englishmen, Dr. Johnson, living in the eighteenth-century Age of Enlightenment, nevertheless spent his last years haunted by the thought that he might be 'one of those who shall be damned'. And once, when visiting his old friend, the Master of Pembroke College, he gave vent 'passionately and loudly' to his terror of being 'sent to Hell, Sir, and punished ever-lastingly'. Few of us are as rational as we think we are, and it may be that even in the twentieth century Lucretius' passionate deter-mination to banish the fear of death is not entirely out of date and unnecessary.

It is by proving the mortality of the soul that Lucretius aims to remove the fear of eternal punishment after death. Therefore he puts together no less than twenty-nine arguments to show that the soul perishes with the body, the first of which the reader will find in extract no. 16.

It is instructive to compare the views of Lucretius with Plato's teaching on the immortality of the soul, put forth with equal conviction and eloquence. Plato's whole thought was dominated by the conviction that the soul is by nature immortal: it existed before our birth, and will continue to exist after our death—while the body is, at best, the soul's transient and unworthy instrument, at worst, a hampering burden from which the philosopher will

---

[1] *Ep.* VII. 27. 1–14. [2] IV. 732–4.

long to be freed. So Socrates is made to speak thus in the *Phaedo*, as he faces his own imminent death:

'The body is the source of endless trouble to us by reason of the mere requirement of food; and is liable also to diseases which overtake and impede us in the search after true being. It fills us full of loves and lusts and fears and fancies of all kinds and endless foolery, and in fact, as men say, takes away from us all power of thinking at all. Whence come wars and fightings and factions? Whence but from the body and the lusts of the body? Wars are occasioned by the love of money, and money has to be acquired for the sake and in the service of the body; and by reason of all these impediments we have no time to give to philosophy; and, last and worst of all, even if we are at leisure to betake ourselves to some speculation, the body is always breaking in upon us, causing turmoil and confusion in our inquiries, and so amazing us that we are prevented from seeing the truth. It has been proved to us by experience that if we would have true knowledge of anything we must be quit of the body. The soul in herself must behold things in themselves; and then we shall attain the wisdom we desire, and of which we say we are lovers; not while we live, but after death; for while in company with the body, the soul cannot have pure knowledge. Knowledge must be attained after death, if at all.'[1]

In this spirit Socrates faces death; and his last words were, according to Plato:[2] 'Crito, I owe a cock to Asclepius; will you remember to pay the debt?' As a man who had recovered from a long illness would sacrifice a cock in gratitude to the god of health, so Socrates is grateful that, for him, life's fever will soon be cured by death, and the living soul made free to soar from the confines of the 'tomb' which is the body.

In face of the rival eloquence of Plato and Lucretius, the reader may well feel himself to be in the position of Buridan's ass, who was placed exactly between two piles of hay and accordingly starved because it could not make up its mind which to choose. But there is a third view which differs from both—that developed by St. Paul in 1 Corinthians xv—on this question of immortality.

[1] Plato, *Phaedo*, 66–7 and 115.
[2] Plato, *Phaedo*, 118A.

Like Lucretius Paul is concerned to rebut the Platonic conception of the body as the soul's temporary instrument. Again like Lucretius he denies the natural immortality of the soul, which cannot exist apart from the body. Paul's conclusion, however, is that the body will be, like Christ's in the Resurrection, 'raised' and 'changed'. There will be a resurrection, but it will not be crudely physical. There will be after death a continuity of existence in a higher form, for which, says Paul, the best analogy is that of a seed which produces its own characteristic plant at death.

None of these three positions can as yet be 'proved', since the weight of rigorously tested evidence is still lacking. All three, with many variations, are current in our contemporary world, though there is no reliable evidence of the relative support given to each. Whether death does mean, as Plato thought, an awakening from the dream of life, or, as Lucretius affirms, an eternal sleep through the dissolution of the personality, or, as in the teaching of Paul and Christianity generally, a continuation of life in inconceivably different and less limiting circumstances, it is incontestably a subject whose greatness demands a corresponding profundity of both thought and expression. In neither of these, the reader will find, has Lucretius failed to rise to the full height of his tremendous theme.

15. In Praise of Epicurus

(III. 1–30)

Lucretius opens the book with the declaration that Epicurus has raised aloft the torch of truth in the surrounding darkness of superstition:

'I am following the footsteps of Epicurus, who first threw light on the true blessings of life. By disclosing the true nature of the universe, he has set men free from superstitious terror. Through his philosophy we see the majestic movement of the atoms in void, the gods in their tranquil abode, but no hell beneath the earth. This vision of reality fills the mind with awe.'

In Praise of Epicurus

E tenebris tantis tam clarum extollere lumen
qui primus potuisti inlustrans commoda vitae,
te sequor, o Graiae gentis decus, inque tuis nunc
ficta pedum pono pressis vestigia signis,
non ita certandi cupidus quam propter amorem   5
quod te imitari aveo; quid enim contendat hirundo
cycnis, aut quidnam tremulis facere artubus haedi
consimile in cursu possint et fortis equi vis?
tu pater es, rerum inventor, tu patria nobis
suppeditas praecepta, tuisque ex, inclute, chartis,   10
floriferis ut apes in saltibus omnia libant,
omnia nos itidem depascimur aurea dicta,
aurea, perpetua semper dignissima vita.
nam simul ac ratio tua coepit vociferari
naturam rerum, divina mente coorta,   15
diffugiunt animi terrores, moenia mundi
discedunt, totum video per inane geri res.
apparet divum numen sedesque quietae
quas neque concutiunt venti nec nubila nimbis
aspergunt neque nix acri concreta pruina   20
cana cadens violat semperque innubilus aether
integit, et large diffuso lumine ridet.
omnia suppeditat porro natura neque ulla
res animi pacem delibat tempore in ullo.
at contra nusquam apparent Acherusia templa   25
nec tellus obstat quin omnia dispiciantur,
sub pedibus quaecumque infra per inane geruntur.
his ibi me rebus quaedam divina voluptas
percipit atque horror, quod sic natura tua vi
tam manifesta patens ex omni parte retecta est.   30

It was not Epicurus, but Leucippus and Democritus, who first invented the atomic system. Epicurus' originality, as Lucretius may be suggesting by *primus* (2), lay in using it to throw light on the 'true blessings of life' (*commoda vitae*).

In somewhat the same way Karl Marx in the nineteenth century used the philosophy of Hegel, which asserted that history develops according to the 'dialectical' process of thesis, antithesis, and synthesis. But whereas Hegel postulated 'spirit' as the motive force behind the process, Marx declared it to be matter. Hence his system was called 'Dialectical Materialism'.

We may be sure, incidentally, that Epicurus and Lucretius would have approved of Marx's making matter all-important (though he used the word in a wider sense than they, to describe the total material conditions of an age). They would also have welcomed his demand that philosophy should be practical. 'The truth, that is, the reality and power of thought, must be demonstrated in practice.'[1] But what would they have made of the famous sentence which comes shortly after: 'Philosophers have only interpreted the world in various ways, but the real task is to alter it'?

By his revelation of the truth about the universe, Epicurus has achieved a twofold blessing for men. First, he has released the mind from the terror of superstition here and now. For the eternal working of atomic law precludes any capricious divine interference in this life; the gods themselves are as 'remote and ineffectual' as Belloc's don. The majestic description of the abode of the gods (18–24) closely follows Homer's lines on Olympus in the *Odyssey*: 'Shaken by no wind, drenched by no showers and invaded by no snows, it is set in a cloudless sea of limpid air with a white radiance playing over all.'[2] Lucretius even patterns his own invented word for 'cloudless', *innubilus*, on Homer's *anephelos* (ἀνέφελος). Vergil reflects this passage of Lucretius: *sedes ubi fata quietas ostendunt*.[3] Tennyson was so impressed that he used it twice, first in *Lucretius*:[4]

---

[1] *Eleven Theses on Feuerbach*, 1845.
[2] VI. 42–6 in E. V. Rieu's translation (Penguin).
[3] *Aeneid* I. 205.   [4] Lines 104–10.

> 'The Gods, who haunt
> The lucid interspace of world and world,
> Where never creeps a cloud, or moves a wind.
> Nor ever falls the least white star of snow,
> Nor ever lowest roll of thunder moans,
> Nor sound of human sorrow mounts to mar
> Their sacred everlasting calm!'

then in *The Passing of Arthur*:[1]

> '. . . the island-valley of Avilion,
> Where falls not hail, or rain, or any snow,
> Nor ever wind blows loudly. . . .'

The second blessing Epicurus has achieved for mankind is to free men from the fear of eternal punishment after death. There is no Acheron beneath the earth, but only the eternal working of atomic law. Lucretius deals more fully with the dread of Acheron in the passage following this extract (31–93), and returns to the topic of everlasting punishment later in the book (extract no. 19). We have already mentioned how the fear of eternal torment preyed on the mind of Dr. Johnson. As late as the end of the nineteenth century, George MacDonald could write a realistic novel, *Robert Falconer*, in which the aged mother bewails her son, who is presumed lost, in these words:

'Gladly would I look upon his dead face, if I could believe that his soul was not among the lost. But oh! the torments of that place and the smoke that goes up forever, smothering the stars. And my Andrew down in the heart of it crying! and me not able to get to him! O Lord, I cannot say thy will be done. But don't lay it to my charge; for if you were a mother yourself, you would not put him there.'

Many would find the last sentence a much more convincing refutation of the doctrine of everlasting punishment after death than the remorseless logic of Lucretius.

[1] Lines 427–9.

16. The Mortality of the Soul
(III. 417–44)

'Mind (*animus*) and soul (*anima*)—the terms may be used inter-changeably—are mortal. For their atomic structure is light and mobile, being quickly moved by even the most insubstantial objects, e.g. images of cloud and smoke. Now just as water, being mobile, flows in all directions when the vessel containing it is broken, so the soul, once the body has disintegrated at death, is quickly dispersed into its component atoms.'

The atoms which compose the soul are, of course, immortal, but, since they are no longer connected with the body, there is no survival of the individual personality.

The passage begins: 'Now consider this next point (*nunc age*), so that you may understand that the minds of living things and their light spirits are born with them (*nativos*) and die with them. . . .' The soul comes into being along with the body, Lucretius asserts, against Plato and others who emphasized the pre-existence of the soul. So, by insisting that the soul is born with the body, Lucretius is providing a further argument that it perishes with the body at death. For ancient thought, as for Hinduism and Buddhism today, immortality refers not only to the future, but also to the past. In G. B. Shaw's *Simpleton of the Unexpected Isles*[1] the Lady Tourist offers to the (Buddhist?) Priest a tract entitled 'Where will you spend eternity?' But a Priestess calls after her, as she departs, 'Where have you spent eternity so far, may I ask? That which has no end can have no beginning.'

Nunc age, nativos animantibus et mortalis
esse animos animasque levis ut noscere possis,
conquisita diu dulcique reperta labore
digna tua pergam disponere carmina vita.   420
tu fac utrumque uno sub iungas nomine eorum,
atque animam verbi causa cum dicere pergam,
mortalem esse docens, animum quoque dicere credas,

[1] Prologue, Scene III.

quatenus est unum inter se coniunctaque res est.
principio quoniam tenuem constare minutis   425
corporibus docui multoque minoribus esse
principiis factam quam liquidus umor aquai
aut nebula aut fumus—nam longe mobilitate
praestat et a tenui causa magis icta movetur;
quippe ubi imaginibus fumi nebulaeque movetur.   430
quod genus in somnis sopiti ubi cernimus alte
exhalare vaporem altaria ferreque fumum;
nam procul haec dubio nobis simulacra geruntur—
nunc igitur quoniam quassatis undique vasis
diffluere umorem et laticem discedere cernis   435
et nebula ac fumus quoniam discedit in auras,
crede animam quoque diffundi multoque perire
ocius et citius dissolvi in corpora prima,
cum semel ex hominis membris ablata recessit.
quippe etenim corpus, quod vas quasi constitit eius,   440
cum cohibere nequit conquassatum ex aliqua re
ac rarefactum detracto sanguine venis,
aere qui credas posse hanc cohiberier ullo,
corpore qui nostro rarus magis incohibens sit?

The picture of the soul disappearing like smoke into the air
(436) goes back to Homer.[1] It was particularly apt to express the
Epicurean conception of the soul's mortality. Interestingly, this
simile is reproduced in the *Wisdom of Solomon*, a biblical
document which was perhaps written at about the same time
as Lucretius' poem, and certainly composed in strong opposition to
the Epicurean position in general, and to this doctrine in particular.
We quote the first verses of chapter ii:

‘For they (i.e. the Epicureans) said within themselves, reasoning not aright, Short and sorrowful is our life; and there is no

[1] *Iliad*, XXIII. 100.

healing when a man cometh to his end, and none was ever known
that gave release from Hades. Because by mere chance were we
born, and hereafter we shall be as though we had never been;
because the breath in our nostrils is as smoke, and while our heart
beateth reason is a spark, which being extinguished, the body
shall be turned to ashes, and the spirit shall be dispersed as thin
air.'[1]

Against this the author then asserts the doctrine of the soul's
immortality, in words so memorable that they often become part
of a funeral service: 'But the souls of the righteous are in the hand
of God, and no torment shall touch them. In the eyes of the foolish
they seem to have died; and their departure was accounted to be
their hurt, and their journeying away from us to be their ruin:
but they are in peace. For even if, in the sight of men, they be
punished, their hope is full of immortality.'[2]

17. The Blessings of Mortality

(III. 830–69)

'Since the soul is mortal, death matters nothing to us. Just as, in
time past, we were not troubled by the Punic Wars, so, in the
future, we shall feel nothing once the union of soul and body
which produces our personal identity is dissolved. Once that
union is destroyed at death, it cannot be renewed, even if the
atoms which constituted it should somehow be reunited. In
infinite time past, the same particles probably co-existed, but we
have no recollection of this. Similarly, it is impossible that we
should feel any ills hereafter, for death makes us as though we
had never been.'

This powerful passage, which combines eloquence with sinewy
argument, might not irreverently be entitled, 'O death, where is
thy sting?' For here Lucretius' determination to banish the 'fear
of something after death' comes to its climax, though, curiously,
he does not mention, as Hamlet does, the feeling that death may
bring relief from life's burdens. He concentrates solely on two

[1] ii. 1–3.   [2] iii. 1–4.

causes which produce the fear of death: first, the belief that something of us will survive to be conscious of suffering; and second, the desire to prolong the pleasures of this life.

It may help to provide an outline of this extract, which contains a lengthy and very important parenthesis. The main argument (830–42 and 862–9) is that 'Death is nothing' because the end of sensation is the end of personal identity. Into this is inserted the long parenthesis (843–61), consisting of two allied arguments. First (843–6): even if the soul, when separated from the body, did have sensation, this is still something completely different from our present consciousness, which depends on the intimate union (*concilium* 805) of soul and body. Second (847–61): it is conceivable that the identical atoms which compose us will at some time again be united. But accepting this as possible (as Epicurus had, but with the proviso that the recombination was purely fortuitous), Lucretius makes it quite clear that this 'reunion' would not be 'us', for we have no memory of such previous existence. The chain of consciousness which makes up our personal identity is decisively snapped at death.

Nil igitur mors est ad nos neque pertinet hilum,   830
quandoquidem natura animi mortalis habetur.
et velut anteacto nil tempore sensimus aegri,
ad confligendum venientibus undique Poenis,
omnia cum belli trepido concussa tumultu
horrida contremuere sub altis aetheris oris,   835
in dubioque fuere utrorum ad regna cadendum
omnibus humanis esset terraque marique,
sic, ubi non erimus, cum corporis atque animai
discidium fuerit quibus e sumus uniter apti,
scilicet haud nobis quicquam, qui non erimus tum,   840
accidere omnino poterit sensumque movere,
non si terra mari miscebitur et mare caelo.
et si iam nostro sentit de corpore postquam
distractast animi natura animaeque potestas,

nil tamen est ad nos qui comptu coniugioque 845
corporis atque animae consistimus uniter apti.
nec, si materiem nostram collegerit aetas
post obitum rursumque redegerit ut sita nunc est
atque iterum nobis fuerint data lumina vitae,
pertineat quicquam tamen ad nos id quoque factum, 850
interrupta semel cum sit repetentia nostri.
et nunc nil ad nos de nobis attinet, ante
qui fuimus, nil iam de illis nos adficit angor.
nam cum respicias immensi temporis omne
praeteritum spatium, tum motus materiai 855
multimodis quam sint, facile hoc accredere possis,
semina saepe in eodem, ut nunc sunt, ordine posta
haec eadem, quibus e nunc nos sumus, ante fuisse.
nec memori tamen id quimus reprehendere mente;
inter enim iectast vitai pausa vageque 860
deerrarunt passim motus ab sensibus omnes.
debet enim, misere si forte aegreque futurumst,
ipse quoque esse in eo tum tempore, cui male possit
accidere. id quoniam mors eximit, esseque probet
illum cui possint incommoda conciliari, 865
scire licet nobis nil esse in morte timendum
nec miserum fieri qui non est posse neque hilum
differre an nullo fuerit iam tempore natus,
mortalem vitam mors cum immortalis ademit.

18. The Futility of Mourning
(III. 894–911)

'It is futile to mourn for a deceased man on the grounds that he
has lost home and family and all that makes life worth living,
since the mortality of the soul ensures that there will be no con-

sciousness of loss. It is equally futile to take the opposite point of view, and contrast the happy state of the departed with the suffering of those who remain. If the dead man is admitted to be free from life's ills, why mourn him so inconsolably?'

In the first line of this extract Bailey places a comma after *laeta*, making *neque uxor optima* go with *occurrent* ('nor your good wife and sweet children run to snatch the first kisses'). Would, however, the comma be better placed after *optima* ('your glad home and good wife will no longer welcome you')? Does the mother join in the race to greet the man of the house as he returns home, or does she stand, waiting to receive him, like the home itself? As most mothers, ancient and modern, contrive to become the most indispensable part of the house, we incline to this latter view. So do Vergil and Gray, it would seem, in their imitation of this passage:

> . . . *dulces pendent circum oscula nati,*
> *casta pudicitiam servat domus* . . . .[1]

> For them no more the blazing hearth shall burn
> Or busy housewife ply her evening care:
> No children run to lisp their sire's return,
> Or climb his knees the envied kiss to share.[2]

In any case, the words provide an attractive glimpse of a natural home life which cannot easily be reconciled with those twin props of the Epicurean way of life, 'self-sufficiency and freedom from disturbance'. Epicurus had made it clear to his followers that it is better not to marry and have children, but presumably he relied on some of them not to follow his advice. For he was extremely fond of children himself, and made a special point of providing in his will for the children of one of his disciples, Metrodorus. This natural desire to provide for others is implied in 897–8 (*tuisque praesidium*), and it is good to know that Epicurus himself was so much more human in practice than his egoistic theory demanded.

---

[1] *Georgics* II. 523–4.   [2] *Elegy*, ll. 21–4.

'Iam iam non domus accipiet te laeta, neque uxor
optima nec dulces occurrent oscula nati　　　　　　895
praeripere et tacita pectus dulcedine tangent.
non poteris factis florentibus esse, tuisque
praesidium. misero misere' aiunt 'omnia ademit
una dies infesta tibi tot praemia vitae.'
illud in his rebus non addunt 'nec tibi earum　　　900
iam desiderium rerum super insidet una.'
quod bene si videant animo dictisque sequantur,
dissoluant animi magno se angore metuque.
'tu quidem ut es leto sopitus, sic eris aevi
quod superest cunctis privatu' doloribus aegris.　　905
at nos horrifico cinefactum te prope busto
insatiabiliter deflevimus, aeternumque
nulla dies nobis maerorem e pectore demet.'
illud ab hoc igitur quaerendum est, quid sit amari
tanto opere, ad somnum si res redit atque quietem,　910
cur quisquam aeterno possit tabescere luctu.

The answer Lucretius gives to the mourner (909–11) seems
cold-blooded. No doubt he had in mind the extravagant expressions of grief put forth by professional mourners and rhetoricians
hired for the occasion. Epicurus himself seems to have taken the
humane view that it is natural to grieve. 'They (the Epicureans)
fight against those who decry grief and tears and lamentations
over the death of friends, and say that the refusal to mourn which
produces indifference arises from another and greater fault, hard-
ness of heart or insatiable craving for notoriety or madness;
therefore it is better to suffer and to grieve.'[1]

　　　　　[1] Plutarch, *Contra Ep. Beat* **XX.** 1101 a.

19. The Hereafter is Here
(III. 978–1023)

'The myths of eternal punishment in Hades are allegories of what happens in this life. For example, Tantalus, Tityus, Sisyphus, and the Danaids are types of people tormented by such passions as fear, desire, ambition, and discontent. Tartarus and the other horrors of the Underworld represent the fear of punishment or the stings of conscience which torture the wrong-doer here on earth.'

Atque ea nimirum quaecumque Acherunte profundo
prodita sunt esse, in vita sunt omnia nobis.
nec miser impendens magnum timet aere saxum   980
Tantalus, ut famast, cassa formidine torpens;
sed magis in vita divum metus urget inanis
mortalis casumque timent quem cuique ferat fors.
nec Tityon volucres ineunt Acherunte iacentem
nec quod sub magno scrutentur pectore quicquam   985
perpetuam aetatem possunt reperire profecto.
quamlibet immani proiectu corporis exstet,
qui non sola novem dispessis iugera membris
obtineat, sed qui terrai totius orbem,
non tamen aeternum poterit perferre dolorem   990
nec praebere cibum proprio de corpore semper.
sed Tityos nobis hic est, in amore iacentem   992
quem volucres lacerant atque exest anxius angor
aut alia quavis scindunt cuppedine curae.
Sisyphus in vita quoque nobis ante oculos est   995
qui petere a populo fascis saevasque securis
imbibit et semper victus tristisque recedit.
nam petere imperium quod inanest nec datur umquam,
atque in eo semper durum sufferre laborem,

hoc est adverso nixantem trudere monte   1000
saxum quod tamen e summo iam vertice rursum
volvitur et plani raptim petit aequora campi.
deinde animi ingratam naturam pascere semper
atque explere bonis rebus satiareque numquam,
quod faciunt nobis annorum tempora, circum   1005
cum redeunt fetusque ferunt variosque lepores,
nec tamen explemur vitai fructibus umquam,
hoc, ut opinor, id est, aevo florente puellas
quod memorant laticem pertusum congerere in vas,
quod tamen expleri nulla ratione potestur.   1010
Cerberus et Furiae iam vero et lucis egestas,
Tartarus horriferos eructans faucibus aestus,
qui neque sunt usquam nec possunt esse profecto.
sed metus in vita poenarum pro male factis   1014
est insignibus insignis, scelerisque luella,   1015
carcer et horribilis de saxo iactu' deorsum,
verbera carnifices robur pix lammina taedae;
quae tamen etsi absunt, at mens sibi conscia factis
praemetuens adhibet stimulos torretque flagellis,
nec videt interea qui terminus esse malorum   1020
possit nec quae sit poenarum denique finis
atque eadem metuit magis haec ne in morte gravescant.
hic Acherusia fit stultorum denique vita.

This view of myth—that it is 'all in the mind'—certainly has a modern ring, and the reader may think immediately of J. P. Sartre's famous play *Huis Clos*, with its much-quoted conclusion 'Hell is other people'.

We cannot give Lucretius or Epicurus the credit for being the first to supply this rational explanation. Several earlier philosophers had seen that myth-making is a process which springs from within man, rather than being simply an explanation of external facts. Thus Democritus anticipates this very passage: 'Some men, not knowing the dissolution of mortal existence, but conscious of evil-doing in this life, spend the time of their life miserably in alarms and fears, inventing false legends about the time after death.'[1]

Several significant modern writers and thinkers can be said to have rediscovered the importance of myth. Thus T. S. Eliot, in his play *The Family Reunion*, makes powerful use of a mythical theme very familiar in Greek tragedy—that of a curse haunting certain families and passing on its taint through the generations till expiation is finally made. In Aeschylus, Sophocles, and Euripides, the hero Orestes is pursued by the Furies who sting his conscience. In Eliot's play the tormented hero struggles with a dread 'deeper than what people call their conscience', until he is brought to realize that he must expiate his parents' sin. In a similar way the French dramatists Anouilh (*Antigone*) and Sartre (*The Flies*) have explored ancient myths. And there are other writers today who seem to be engaged in inventing myths: as, for example, Samuel Beckett in *Waiting for Godot* and William Golding in *The Spire*.

Lucretius would doubtless have been puzzled that outstanding and creative writers should accept his explanation of myths and yet continue to use them twenty centuries later. But he wrote without benefit of the various researches into the unconscious mind initiated by Freud, and elaborated by C. G. Jung (a one-time disciple of Freud and founder of 'Analytical Psychology') into what he called 'A Science of Mythology'. Jung saw myths as the expression of man's deepest feelings and experiences; hence they are a part of what he calls the 'collective unconscious'. They give expression to fundamental hopes and fears, and are the source, not only of dread, but of creativity. They are 'the hidden treasure upon which mankind ever and anon has drawn, and from which it has raised up its gods and demons, and all those potent and mighty thoughts without which man ceases to be man'.[2] If this is so, we need not wonder why philosophers have had such scant success in their attempts, however rational, to 'explain away' myths.

[1] Diels, B 297.   [2] *Two Essays on Analytical Psychology*, p. 66.

BOOK IV

MUCH of this book is concerned with the Epicurean theory of knowledge. A philosophical system must not rest content with the question 'What is the nature of supreme reality?' but must proceed to ask 'How do we know that reality?' For Epicurus reality was simply atoms falling in void. His theory of knowledge was equally straightforward. It accepted the evidence of the senses and dismissed all mystical and idealist approaches. Epicureanism was diametrically opposed to such philosophies as Heraclitus' (sixth century B.C.), who said, 'The senses are bad witnesses to men if their souls be not pure', and to Plato, who held that nothing worth calling knowledge could be derived from the senses. They, at best, could only admit men to the twilight world of 'opinion', according to Plato. True knowledge, as the soaring prose of the *Phaedo*, Book VII of the *Republic*, and the *Theaetetus* proclaims, is of the eternal, supra-sensible world of the 'ideas' or 'forms' which only the soul, untrammelled by the senses, can hope to see. After the mystical heights of Plato's 'idealist' theory of knowledge the Epicurean system is very much down to earth. Things are more or less what they seem, it says; all knowledge without exception comes through the senses, and sensation itself is infallible, for whatever is perceived must exist.

This has seemed to some a satisfying and refreshingly sensible account of how we know reality. Others have seen it as a delusory simplification of the problem at the expense of half the facts. In modern philosophy the most fascinating attempts so far to grapple with the problem of knowledge were those of the three British philosophers of the eighteenth century, Locke, Berkeley, and Hume. Locke (1632–1704), in his *Essay Concerning Human Understanding*, starts from a position similar to the Epicurean and totally opposed to that of Plato. He is at pains to prove that all knowledge is derived from experience. 'Let us then suppose the mind to be, as we say, white paper, void of all characters, without any ideas; how comes it to be furnished? Whence comes it by that vast store, which the busy and boundless fancy of man has painted on it with an almost endless variety? Whence has it all the materials of reason and knowledge? To this I answer in one word, from experience; in that all our knowledge is founded, and from that it ultimately derives itself.'[1] This is just the position that 'common sense' in all ages has approved. But it is not without difficulties. In particular, it assumes that mental occurrences, which we call sensations, have causes outside themselves, and that these causes more or less resemble the sensations. But what we actually experience is the sensations, not their causes. How can we prove, from experience, that this mental experience does not arise from within the mind itself?

Bishop Berkeley (1685–1753) arrived at just this position in *The Principles of Human Knowledge*. For 'the reality of sensible things consists in their being perceived', and 'whatever is immediately perceived is an idea; and can any idea exist out of the mind?' He then proceeds to the paradoxical position that only minds and mental events can exist, and that the material world is unreal.

Hume (1711–76) accepted Berkeley's abolition of matter, and, in his *Treatise of Human Nature*, reached the sceptical conclusion that we have knowledge only of our own impressions and ideas. Our apparent consciousness of ourselves is as delusive as our apparent awareness of objects out there. Nothing is to be learned of the outside world from observation or sense-perception. We cannot help believing something about reality, but all belief is equally irrational. 'If we believe that fire warms or water refreshes, 'tis only because it costs us too much pains to think otherwise.' So we reach the sceptical conclusion, which seems to start from Epicurus' own premiss but ends at a wholly contradictory position. 'All probable reasoning is nothing but a species of sensation. 'Tis not solely in poetry and music we must follow our taste and sentiment, but likewise in philosophy. When I am convinced of any principle, 'tis only an idea, which strikes more strongly upon me. When I give the preference to one set of arguments above another, I do nothing but decide from my feeling concerning the superiority of their influence. Objects have no discoverable

[1] Book II, Chapter 1, Section 2.

connexion together; nor is it from any other principle but custom operating upon the imagination, that we can draw any inference from the appearance of one to the existence of another.'[1]

This scepticism concerning the possibility of real knowledge so shocked the great Prussian philosopher, Immanuel Kant (1724–1804), that it aroused him, as he said, from his 'dogmatic slumber'. He spent twelve years of concentrated thought on the problem, allowing himself only a brief afternoon walk each day as a diversion. At the end of this period he wrote his most celebrated work, *The Critique of Pure Reason*. Clearly he believed his prolonged and rigorous thought had been effective, for he wrote in the preface to the first edition of his book: 'I venture to assert that there is not a single metaphysical problem which has not been solved, or for the solution of which at least the key has not been supplied.' Kant's solution to the problem of knowledge is that there is an outside world which causes sensations, but that the mind inevitably orders and interprets these sense-data. The 'things in themselves' which cause the sensations are strictly unknowable. But in the act of perception our minds bring to the situation such categories as space, time, quantity, and quality, which enable us to have the mental experience of knowing. These categories are a part of our perception, and not of the world outside. We experience reality only by looking through the coloured glasses—perhaps we should say the darkened glasses—of perception.

So Kant solved the problem of knowledge, to his own satisfaction. But his confidence was as premature as that of Epicurus and Lucretius. For the question 'How do we know reality?' still engrosses philosophers, the more so as the other question 'What is ultimate reality?' has increasingly been taken over by scientists. A glance at the contents of such periodicals as *Mind* or *The Journal of Philosophy* will show how important the problem of knowledge is for modern philosophy. An attempt to read any of the articles will probably convince the student that it is also exceedingly difficult. Though modern philosophers employ a much more sophisticated and technical logic than Epicurus and Lucretius, or than Locke, Berkeley, and Hume, they cannot yet

[1] Book I, Part 3, Section 8.

be said to have solved the problem of knowledge, any more than Kant did, despite massive intellectual effort. It may be that much help will be forthcoming from the young science of psychology. Meanwhile, despite the naïveté of the Epicurean account, the reader will find much shrewd reasoning, sound observation, and plenty of philosophic difficulty in the following extracts, all of which are concerned in one way or another with the question 'How do we know reality?'

20. Sensation the Basis of all Perception

(IV. 26–43)

'Having shown the nature of the soul,[1] I now proceed to demonstrate the existence of 'images'—a sort of outer skin which peels off from the surface of objects and flies through the air. It is their impact which alarms us as we sleep with the notion that they are ghosts from Hades. This alarm is unnecessary, as I have already shown that soul and body dissolve into their component atoms at death.'

Starting from the general position that all perception is through the senses, Lucretius now sets out to state the Epicurean theory of vision, viz. that it is caused by the 'images' striking the eye of the beholder; but at line 33, distracted by the need to deliver a blow at his old enemy, the belief in survival after death, he turns aside from this main task and passes on to the special case of visions of the dead.

Atque animi quoniam docui natura quid esset
et quibus e rebus cum corpore compta vigeret
quove modo distracta rediret in ordia prima,
nunc agere incipiam tibi, quod vementer ad has res
attinet, esse ea quae rerum simulacra vocamus;   30
quae, quasi membranae summo de corpore rerum
dereptae, volitant ultroque citroque per auras,

[1] See commentary on extract no. 16, p. 52.

atque eadem nobis vigilantibus obvia mentis
terrificant atque in somnis, cum saepe figuras
contuimur miras simulacraque luce carentum,   35
quae nos horrifice languentis saepe sopore
excierunt, ne forte animas Acherunte reamur
effugere aut umbras inter vivos volitare
neve aliquid nostri post mortem posse relinqui,
cum corpus simul atque animi natura perempta   40
in sua discessum dederint primordia quaeque.
dico igitur rerum effigias tenuisque figuras
mittier ab rebus summo de corpore eorum.

Later on (54 sqq.) Lucretius provides vivid analogies for this
difficult concept of vision through images, such as that of the
snake sloughing its skin or a mirror reflecting light. For a system
like Epicureanism sight is obviously the most difficult of the
senses to explain. No such difficulty, for example, arises with taste,
where it is the direct physical contact between the object and the
tongue or palate which clearly causes the sensation. Early Greek
philosophers had been interested in the phenomenon of sight,
and Empedocles had suggested that an 'effluence' from the seen
object must impinge upon the eye. The atomists had accepted the
existence of such effluences, adding that they must, of course, be
composed of atoms. This is the view that Epicurus takes over and
elaborates and which Lucretius follows.

21. Optical Illusions

(IV. 379–403)

'In the case of optical illusions, it is not our eyes that are deceived.
Their function is to see; it is for the mind to interpret what is
seen, and this is where deception comes in. For example, when
we are on a moving ship, it may seem to be stationary, while ships
at anchor, and the shore itself, may seem to move. Just so with the

sun and stars. And widely separated hills appear linked together
when seen from a great distance at sea. In the same way children,
after spinning round themselves, seem to perceive everything
around them whirling and tottering.'

This extract is part of a long passage describing a large number
of optical illusions. Immediately before it begins, Lucretius was
dealing with the illusion that our shadow is an object which follows us as we walk, whereas really it is the absence of sunlight at
successive points along the ground: *hic* in line 379 ('herein')
refers to this.

Nec tamen hic oculos falli concedimus hilum.
nam quocumque loco sit lux atque umbra tueri   380
illorum est; eadem vero sint lumina necne,
umbraque quae fuit hic eadem nunc transeat illuc,
an potius fiat paulo quod diximus ante,
hoc animi demum ratio discernere debet,
nec possunt oculi naturam noscere rerum.   385
proinde animi vitium hoc oculis adfingere noli.
qua vehimur navi, fertur, cum stare videtur;
quae manet in statione, ea praeter creditur ire.
et fugere ad puppim colles campique videntur
quos agimus praeter navem velisque volamus.   390
sidera cessare aetheriis adfixa cavernis
cuncta videntur, et assiduo sunt omnia motu,
quandoquidem longos obitus exorta revisunt,
cum permensa suo sunt caelum corpore claro.
solque pari ratione manere et luna videtur   395
in statione, ea quae ferri res indicat ipsa.
exstantisque procul medio de gurgite montis
classibus inter quos liber patet exitus ingens,
insula coniunctis tamen ex his una videtur.
atria versari et circumcursare columnae   400

usque adeo fit uti pueris videantur, ubi ipsi
desierunt verti, vix ut iam credere possint
non supra sese ruere omnia tecta minari.

If all perception is through sensation, what account can be given
of misperception? The Epicurean explanation is shrewd and by
no means wide of the mark. It distinguishes between two processes in perception. The first is sensation, which is the passive
reception of images by the sense-organ concerned (in this extract,
the eye). The second is the active process of perception, in which
the mind itself interprets the material presented to it by the senses,
through its own general concepts and expectations. Thus, in the
case of optical illusions, it is not the eyes which are deceived, but
the mind which makes false inferences.

If we would avoid such illusion, say Epicurus and Lucretius,
then we must accept each image presented by our eyes only as an
hypothesis awaiting confirmation or disproof. What seems to be
a round tower when seen at a distance may turn out to be a
square one; so a rigorous suspension of judgement is continually
called for. A good Epicurean would appreciate the story of the
two men, one a scientist and the other a farmer, who were travelling by train through the countryside. Seeing a flock of bare-
looking sheep in a field, the farmer said to his friend, 'Look: those
sheep have recently been sheared.' The scientist gazed fixedly at
them for as long as possible as the train sped by, then cautiously
replied, 'Yes, they do seem to have been—on this side at any rate.'

This separation of sensation from perception was accepted by
almost all psychology in the last century. It was taken for granted
that sensation was the experience we have when the sensory areas
of the brain are stimulated, while perception meant the addition
of ideas, images, and memories derived from past experience.
Thus, seeing a house would involve two processes: first, the
reception of an oblong shape; and second, the attribution of
various qualities to it, such as depth, area, rooms, doors, etc. This
accords well with the Epicurean view and with 'common sense'.
But is it true?

One particular school of psychology in this century has

vigorously affirmed that sensation and perception cannot be thus separated in fact; that the awareness of pattern or structure in sense-data is innate, not learnt. A baby does not start, as we might think, with a chaos of individual sensations and gradually learn by experience to group these individual elements together into a whole, thus achieving perception as though fitting together the separate pieces of a jigsaw puzzle. Right from the start we perceive a whole structure, not an aggregate of parts. Even a totally unfamiliar object will be seen not as a jumble of disconnected sensations but as a form or figure.

Though evidence from babies themselves is hard to come by, the views of this, the Gestalt school of psychology (*Gestalt* means 'pattern'), are rapidly gaining acceptance. They are supported by the experience of people born blind who have afterwards gained their sight. Such patients perceive an organized, related sense-field as soon as they see at all; though they do not, of course, immediately recognize objects for what they are. It would seem that sensation and perception can be separated only in theory and not in experience. This the reader may verify by considering the appended figures. He will inevitably group together lines *a* and *b*, then *c* and *d*, etc. Again, he will see the left-hand group of dots as vertical rows and the right-hand group as horizontal rows.

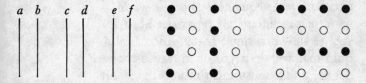

22. Sensation the Basis of all Knowledge

(IV. 469–84)

'Complete scepticism is an impossible position, for a man who says that nothing can be known is admitting that he does not know whether knowledge is possible. And whence does he derive the concept of truth? It is actually derived from the senses, and what more certain standard have we than they? Reason itself cannot invalidate their testimony, for reason is wholly derived from them.'

This was a stock refutation of scepticism in antiquity, and is still valid against the extreme form, 'absolute scepticism'. If the absolute sceptic affirms 'Nothing can be known', it is open to the objector to reply: 'But this itself is a proposition, which, presumably, you think can be known; therefore the possibility of some form of knowledge exists.' If the sceptic retreats to the position of being merely uncertain whether anything can be known, he has abandoned absolute scepticism.

Denique nil sciri siquis putat, id quoque nescit
an sciri possit, quoniam nil scire fatetur.   470
hunc igitur contra mittam contendere causam,
qui capite ipse sua in statuit vestigia sese.
et tamen hoc quoque uti concedam scire, at id ipsum
quaeram, cum in rebus veri nil viderit ante,
unde sciat quid sit scire et nescire vicissim,   475
notitiam veri quae res falsique crearit
et dubium certo quae res differre probarit.
invenies primis ab sensibus esse creatam
notitiem veri neque sensus posse refelli.
nam maiore fide debet reperirier illud,   480
sponte sua veris quod possit vincere falsa.
quid maiore fide porro quam sensus haberi
debet? an ab sensu falso ratio orta valebit
dicere eos contra, quae tota ab sensibus orta est?

The most famous of ancient sceptics was Pyrrho of Elis (360–270 B.C.). He is said to have maintained that it is impossible to know things as they are and that there can be no rational grounds for preferring one course of action to another (which was much the position adopted by Hume).[1] This dogmatic scepticism had a considerable popular appeal in the unsettled world of the third

[1] See p. 63.

century B.C., and it is not uncommon in our own unsettled century, when it usually takes the form of a misunderstanding of relativity. 'Since all knowledge is relative,' it asserts, 'we can be sure of nothing.'

Scepticism must be carefully distinguished from the much more moderate position of 'agnosticism'. Scepticism says: 'Nobody knows, and nobody can ever know.' Agnosticism says: 'I don't know; I suspend judgement.'

23. Images in Sleep

(IV. 1011–23)

'Men experience in dreams the emotions connected with the activities of waking life. Sometimes there are dreams of violent activities like battle and capture, sometimes nightmares of dying which startle the sleeper into wakefulness.'

Porro hominum mentes, magnis quae motibus edunt
magna, itidem saepe in somnis faciuntque geruntque,
reges expugnant, capiuntur, proelia miscent,
tollunt clamorem, quasi si iugulentur, ibidem.
multi depugnant gemitusque doloribus edunt   1015
et quasi pantherae morsu saevive leonis
mandantur magnis clamoribus omnia complent.
multi de magnis per somnum rebu' loquuntur
indicioque sui facti persaepe fuere.
multi mortem obeunt. multi, de montibus altis   1020
ut qui praecipitent ad terram corpore toto,
exterruntur et ex somno quasi mentibu' capti
vix ad se redeunt permoti corporis aestu.

Dreams are a sort of perception, and, as such, have been of considerable interest to philosophers (as well as to ordinary folk, who are usually as ready to describe their dreams as their friends are to hear them). Modern interest has acquired scientific status through the researches of Freud, who, in his most famous work, *The Interpretation of Dreams*, proved that 'dreams are the royal road to the unconscious'. The reader will not expect the Epicureans to have anticipated the insights of psycho-analysis, but there are some interesting points of similarity between the Epicurean and modern views.

For Epicurus and Lucretius there is a part of the mind which is still active even when consciousness is withdrawn in sleep, which can still be influenced by external impressions, i.e. the 'images'.[1] But for psycho-analysis of course the source of this activity of the unconscious is not external impressions but the inner demands of instinctual desires, held down in waking existence but springing to life in dreams. We need go no further into the Freudian view that all dreams are 'wish fulfilments'—a view stoutly challenged by Professor H. J. Eysenck (e.g. in the entertaining chapter entitled 'The Interpretation of Dreams' of his book *Sense and Nonsense in Psychology*). It would need all the resources of Freudian symbolism, incidentally, to make the examples of dreams given in this passage into wish fulfilments.

Another point of interest in the Epicurean view is its opposition to what might be called the 'prophetic' interpretation of dreams, so universally popular in ancient times, and not altogether outgrown in civilized societies. This assumes that dreams are meant to reveal something about the future. In the book of Genesis Pharaoh's dream of the fat and lean kine inevitably foreshadows the prosperous and lean years that are to come. In the *Iliad*, when the Greek army before Troy was smitten by a pestilence, Achilles suggested that guidance for the future should be obtained from dreams, 'for dreams descend from Zeus'.[2] According to Levy-Bruhl, there are still primitive societies where, if a man dreams that he owns someone else's property, the owner will say to him, 'Take it; it is yours', so inevitable is the dream's fulfilment. By contrast the Epicurean account of dreams is (like Freud's) rational and scientific. It seeks their meaning through looking into the causes which preceded them in the past, not by looking

[1] Cf. extract no. 20.   [2] I. 63.

to them to throw light upon the future. Dreams, as Lucretius here shows, vividly reproduce the past events and problems which are still 'on our mind'; they do not point to the future.

It may be added that something like the 'prophetic' view can still be found in the works of Jung, and also in J. W. Dunne's book *An Experiment with Time*. And the most famous example of faith in the problem-solving virtues of the dream is the story of how the German scientist Kekulé formed his conception of the benzene ring, which revolutionized organic chemistry. He was writing a text-book of chemistry. 'But it did not go well . . . I turned the chair to the fireplace and sank into a half-sleep. The atoms flitted before my eyes . . . wriggling and turning like snakes. And see, what was that? One of the snakes seized its own tail and the image whirled scornfully before my eyes. As though from a flash of lightning I awoke. I occupied the rest of the night in working out the consequences of the hypothesis. Let us learn to dream, gentlemen.'[1]

[1] W. Beveridge, *The Art of Scientific Investigation*, p. 56.

BOOK V

THE last two books of the *De Rerum Natura* form an extended appendix to Lucretius' main argument, which is now complete.

He has shown that the ultimate explanation of reality is to be derived, not from the interference of gods, but from atoms falling in void (Book I); and that all compound objects are built up from these basic materials (Book II). He has described the nature of the soul and its mortality (Book III), and propounded the Epicurean theory of knowledge (Book IV). Now he proceeds powerfully to underline his argument by asserting that the world and human life owe nothing to the design of the gods, but have slowly, painfully, and even accidentally, evolved.

In setting forth his argument for a slow and random development of all things, as against a once-for-all creation according to plan, Lucretius inevitably reminds us of the Darwinian theory of Evolution, which has so powerfully influenced our whole climate of thought in the hundred years since it was first promulgated There is, of course, in the Epicurean speculative system as here expounded by Lucretius no more than the faintest of fore-shadowings of Darwin's great discovery. But that system did range itself determinedly against the 'argument from design', which nevertheless triumphantly held the field until Darwin's careful observations and scientifically verifiable hypothesis provided a much more decisive challenge, some twenty centuries after Lucretius. This fact makes it worth while briefly to trace the course of evolutionary thought, and to consider how and in what sense it can be said to have destroyed the argument from design.

Among the early Greek philosophers Anaximander (610–547 B.C.) postulated an indeterminate primordial matter as a basis for cosmic and organic development. He concluded, from the evidence of fossils, which showed that the sea had once covered a much greater area of land, that this material was watery. Heraclitus (*c.* 510 B.C.), amid a welter of enigmatic and speculative utterances, emphasized the idea of conflict among living organisms.

But these speculations were not followed up in the ancient world by any philosophers but the Epicureans. The most influential Greek philosophers, Plato and Aristotle, were much more concerned with final causes: i.e. the question they sought to answer was 'What purpose does the universe or any particular part of it serve?', not 'How does it come to be thus? What causes preceded it?' In addition the early centuries of the Christian era saw the general acceptance by Christian thinkers of the ideas of special creation and the fixity of species, as described in the early chapters of Genesis. Even as late as the eighteenth century, the great Linnaeus, to whom we owe the concept of genus and species, stated firmly that there could be no such thing as a new species.

It was in the late eighteenth and early nineteenth centuries that thinkers in several fields began to move away from this static outlook. The French biologist Buffon (1707–88) pointed out that competition for survival might cause one species to replace another in time. Erasmus Darwin (1751–1802), the grandfather of Charles Darwin, discussed the possibility that environmental changes, such as differing climates, might cause far-reaching changes in plants and animals. At the same time the economist Malthus grimly predicted a world struggle for survival among human beings, as populations expanded faster than the means of supporting them. And geologists like Sir Charles Lyell showed that changes in the earth's surface could best be explained by the operation of natural forces over a long period of time.

These varied evolutionary ideas crystallized in Charles Darwin's theory of 'descent with modification through natural selection'. His hypothesis was, first, that there is chance variation in living organisms, and second, that natural selection operates upon this process through the survival of the fittest. The mechanism of that selection, which forms the subject-matter of Genetics, does not concern us here. But it is hardly open to doubt that evolution in Darwin's sense has occurred; creation was not a once-for-all act, and the species are not fixed. What ancient philosophers like Epicurus and Lucretius had vaguely speculated about, Darwin proved by his immensely careful collection of facts and remorseless scientific inquiry.

Does this mean the end of the argument from design, which has meant so much to the average thoughtful person who thinks he sees order as well as beauty in the universe? If one is stirred, as Lucretius himself must have been when he wrote the opening lines of Book I, by the wonder of spring in the countryside, it is hard to believe that all this is no more than the accidental collocation of atoms. Again, the human capacity to create satisfying relations with other human beings (which Lucretius celebrates in Book V as the crown of human development)—all that is summed up in the ideas of civilization and culture—it is hard to reconcile this with the blundering and random growth of human society which evolutionary thought would suggest and which Lucretius' account is at pains to depict.

The argument from design in its naïve eighteenth-century form, which thought of the universe as a piece of intricate mechanism like a watch, and argued from that to an Eternal Watchmaker who had set it going at Creation, is clearly unacceptable. But it is at least possible that the opposite extreme of randomness may prove untenable. Is it possible, by random variation, to account for such an incredibly complex entity as the human eye, with its 137,000,000 separate seeing elements spread out in the sheet of the retina? Even when the vast expanse of geological time is granted, will it provide enough aeons to account for the evolution of the human brain without recourse to some concept of purpose?

Darwin himself was aware of this dilemma, and wrote to his friend Gray: 'I am conscious that I am in a hopeless muddle. I cannot think that the world as we see it is the result of chance, and yet I cannot look upon each separate thing as the result of design.' But Neo-Darwinians are made of sterner stuff, and Sir Julian Huxley asserts: 'The purpose manifested in evolution, whether in adaptation, specialization, or biological progress, is only an apparent purpose. . . . It is we who have read purpose into evolution, as earlier men projected will and emotion into inorganic phenomena like storm or earthquake.'[1] The words might almost have been written by Lucretius, and the sentiment is

---

[1] *Evolution, the Modern Synthesis*, p. 578.

certainly his. But the argument for purpose in the universe and a creative Mind controlling evolution has had its powerful supporters, notably the late C. E. Raven in his Gifford Lectures 1952–3 on *Science and Religion*, and in a previous smaller work, *Science, Religion and the Future*, from which we quote: 'If the universe of our experience is studied and described as a whole, it displays a continuous process, neither mechanical in its operation nor inevitable in its outcome, but nevertheless moving, with a vast and impressive impulse, towards a recognizable if remote end, . . . the fully personal life which is its goal.'

The ensuing extracts will show that the ancient argument in which Epicurus and Lucretius engaged is also surprisingly modern. The outcome of that argument is at least as important to us it was to them.

24. The Imperfection of the World

(V. 195–234)

'Even without knowledge of the atomic theory we can see that the world is too faulty to be of divine origin. Half of it is occupied by mountains, forests filled with wild beasts, rocks, marshes and seas. Two thirds of the rest are useless to man because of their excessive heat and cold. Much of the remainder is wild and needs immense labour to bring it under cultivation. Mankind itself is constantly menaced by wild beasts, disease, untimely death. Consider, also, the general helplessness of the human infant compared with the offspring of animals.'

Quod si iam rerum ignorem primordia quae sint,   195
hoc tamen ex ipsis caeli rationibus ausim
confirmare aliisque ex rebus reddere multis,
nequaquam nobis divinitus esse paratam
naturam rerum: tanta stat praedita culpa.
principio quantum caeli tegit impetus ingens,   200
inde avidam partem montes silvaeque ferarum

possedere, tenent rupes vastaeque paludes
et mare quod late terrarum distinet oras.
inde duas porro prope partis fervidus ardor
assiduusque geli casus mortalibus aufert.   205
quod superest arvi, tamen id natura sua vi
sentibus obducat, ni vis humana resistat
vitai causa valido consueta bidenti
ingemere et terram pressis proscindere aratris.
si non fecundas vertentes vomere glebas   210
terraique solum subigentes cimus ad ortus,
sponte sua nequeant liquidas exsistere in auras;
et tamen interdum magno quaesita labore
cum iam per terras frondent atque omnia florent,
aut nimiis torret fervoribus aetherius sol   215
aut subiti peremunt imbres gelidaeque pruinae,
flabraque ventorum violento turbine vexant.
praeterea genus horriferum natura ferarum
humanae genti infestum terraque marique
cur alit atque auget? cur anni tempora morbos   220
apportant? quare mors immatura vagatur?
tum porro puer, ut saevis proiectus ab undis
navita, nudus humi iacet, infans, indigus omni
vitali auxilio, cum primum in luminis oras
nixibus ex alvo matris natura profudit,   225
vagituque locum lugubri complet, ut aequumst
cui tantum in vita restet transire malorum.
at variae crescunt pecudes armenta feraeque
nec crepitacillis opus est nec cuiquam adhibendast
almae nutricis blanda atque infracta loquella   230
nec varias quaerunt vestis pro tempore caeli,
denique non armis opus est, non moenibus altis,

qui sua tutentur, quando omnibus omnia large
tellus ipsa parit naturaque daedala rerum.

Lucretius begins his systematic attack on the argument from design with a double blow:

1. The world itself, he asserts, contains obvious imperfections. There is ugliness as well as beauty, much that is purposeless and cruel besides apparent purpose. This is a legitimate criticism of the too cosy view of the providential ordering of the universe which supposes that 'all is for the best in this best possible of worlds'.

2. Man is constantly menaced by a largely hostile environment. He is subject to suffering and sudden death, and his frailty is epitomized by the sheer helplessness of the human infant. Again, this is a telling count against any over-sentimental view of the human condition. Yet Lucretius' description is realistic rather than pessimistic. Others have gone much farther. Lord Russell, for example, in his famous essay 'A Free Man's Worship',[1] starts from a similar position to that of Lucretius, but reaches a far more sombre conclusion:

'Such in outline, but even more purposeless, more void of meaning, is the world which Science presents for our belief. Amid such a world, if anywhere, our ideals must find a home. That man is the product of causes which had no prevision of the end they were achieving; that his origin, his growth, his hopes and fears, his loves and his beliefs, are but the outcome of accidental collocations of atoms; that no fire, no heroism, no intensity of thought and feeling, can preserve an individual life beyond the grave; that all the labours of the ages, all the devotion, all the inspiration, all the noonday brightness of human genius are destined to extinction in the vast death of the solar system, and that the whole temple of man's achievement must inevitably be buried beneath the debris of a universe in ruins—all these things, if not quite beyond dispute, are yet so nearly certain that no philosophy which rejects them can hope to stand. Only within the scaffolding of these truths, only on a firm foundation of unyielding despair, can the soul's habitation henceforth be safely built.'

[1] *Mysticism and Logic*, p. 47.

25. How the World Arose

(V. 416–31)

'The formation of the earth, sky, sea, and planets was not by design but by chance, after the endless collisions, the random meetings and combinations of atoms.'

Sed quibus ille modis coniectus materiai
fundarit terram et caelum pontique profunda,
solis lunai cursus, ex ordine ponam.
nam certe neque consilio primordia rerum
ordine se suo quaeque sagaci mente locarunt   420
nec quos quaeque darent motus pepigere profecto,
sed quia multa modis multis primordia rerum
ex infinito iam tempore percita plagis
ponderibusque suis consuerunt concita ferri
omnimodisque coire atque omnia pertemptare   425
quaecumque inter se possent congressa creare,
propterea fit uti magnum vulgata per aevum
omne genus coetus et motus experiundo
tandem conveniant ea quae convecta repente
magnarum rerum fiunt exordia saepe,   430
terrai maris et caeli generisque animantum.

Lucretius is here concerned, not to describe in detail how the world arose, but to deny those views which ascribe purpose to the process. The Stoics, with their concept of the *anima mundi*, and above all Plato, strongly emphasized such providential design as Lucretius intends to refute. Here is Plato's account of Creation:[1]

'Now let us say why the great Architect designed creation and this universe. He was good, and no jealousy about anything is ever found in the good. So, being quite free from it, he wished to make everything as far as possible good like himself. . . . He

[1] *Timaeus* 29D–30C.

found the whole visible world, not in a state of rest, but moving at random and in no order. . . . So, as he considered the matter, he began to find that in the whole of visible nature there was simply nothing without mind that was ever going to be superior to anything with mind, and also that it is impossible that anything should have mind without soul. On the strength of this consideration, he began to contrive the universe by attaching mind to soul and soul to body, thus producing what is beautiful and good.'

This description, beautiful though it is, moves in the realm of myth and fantasy, like the Genesis accounts. The picture which Lucretius presents is a chaos of material fragments, the atoms, flying, spinning, colliding, combining and re-combining, until, after almost endless random movement, our world somehow emerges. And this is a good deal nearer the truth than Plato or the Stoics got in the ancient world, or those eighteenth-century philosophers and theologians who saw the universe as a watch and God as the Almighty Watchmaker who set the orderly mechanism going.

How *did* the world begin? It is by no means certain, but, if we accept the view of Professor F. Hoyle in *Frontiers of Astronomy*, it would seem that it all started from a cloud of inter-stellar gas which condensed through the forces of gravity into stars. One particular star became a vast nuclear furnace, splitting up the nuclei of atoms and building up new and complex elements. Finally, when its inner temperature reached five thousand million degrees centigrade, it collapsed and caused a cataclysmic explosion. As it shattered, atoms of all the elements which had been created during its development tore outwards through space, forming again a huge cloud of gas. One fragment of the cloud condensed to become our sun with a whirling disc around it like a halo. This disc moved outward from the sun, and, as it did so, 'substances condensed out of the gas as a swarm of solid bodies'. These small solid bodies combined to form larger bodies. At last, from a myriad incoherent fragments, there emerged four spheres circling the sun: Mercury, Venus, Mars, and our Earth.

We can imagine that Lucretius, had he been able to hear this scientific account of creation, would have remarked with considerable satisfaction, 'That proves my point.' The whole process of the Earth's formation looks random enough, even casual. Yet Professor Hoyle has this also to say:

'Now was this an accident? . . . I believe that nothing arbitrary entered into the chain of incident that connected the origin of the Earth, and of living creatures on the Earth, with the general march of cosmic events.'[1]

And again: 'It has been stated by some that only as a result of a series of prodigious accidents were conditions made suitable for the development of life on the Earth. It was not an accident that the small planets were formed nearest the sun. Nor do the compositions of the planets seem in the least to be a matter of chance.'[2]

Professor Hoyle does not elaborate these statements, and we should hesitate to quote them in support of any argument from design. Nevertheless, taken at their face value, they would seem to leave the door open, as Lucretius does not, for some sort of purposiveness in creation.

26. Early Man

(V. 925–61)

'Primitive men were hardier and bigger than we. They lived like wild beasts, roaming at large, with no knowledge of agriculture, but feeding on acorns and berries, and drinking from rivers and streams. They did not know the use of fire or clothing, lived in woods or caves, and had no common life and laws.'

At genus humanum multo fuit illud in arvis   925
durius, ut decuit, tellus quod dura creasset,
et maioribus et solidis magis ossibus intus
fundatum, validis aptum per viscera nervis,
nec facile ex aestu nec frigore quod caperetur
nec novitate cibi nec labi corporis ulla.   930

[1] Op. cit., p. 96.   [2] Op. cit., p. 105.

multaque per caelum solis volventia lustra
vulgivago vitam tractabant more ferarum.
nec robustus erat curvi moderator aratri
quisquam, nec scibat ferro molirier arva
nec nova defodere in terram virgulta neque altis   935
arboribus veteres decidere falcibu' ramos.
quod sol atque imbres dederant, quod terra crearat
sponte sua, satis id placabat pectora donum.
glandiferas inter curabant corpora quercus
plerumque; et quae nunc hiberno tempore cernis   940
arbita puniceo fieri matura colore,
plurima tum tellus etiam maiora ferebat.
multaque praeterea novitas tum florida mundi
pabula dura tulit, miseris mortalibus ampla.
at sedare sitim fluvii fontesque vocabant,   945
ut nunc montibus e magnis decursus aquai
claricitat late sitientia saecla ferarum.
denique nota vagis silvestria templa tenebant
nympharum, quibus e scibant umori' fluenta
lubrica proluvie largā lavere umida saxa,   950
umida saxa, super viridi stillantia musco,
et partim plano scatĕre atque erumpere campo.
necdum res igni scibant tractare neque uti
pellibus et spoliis corpus vestire ferarum,
sed nemora atque cavos montis silvasque colebant   955
et frutices inter condebant squalida membra
verbera ventorum vitare imbrisque coacti.
nec commune bonum poterant spectare neque ullis
moribus inter se scibant nec legibus uti.
quod cuique obtulerat praedae fortuna, ferebat   960
sponte sua sibi quisque valere et vivere doctus.

The realism of this condensed description is remarkable when one considers that almost all classical writers assumed, like the Book of Genesis, that primitive man lived in a golden age in the remote past. Here is an Eleatic philosopher speaking in Plato's dialogue *The Statesman*:

'God used to feed and tend people himself, just as men, being animals, but more like God than the rest, act as herdsmen to other animals inferior to themselves. And when God was their shepherd, there were no organized communities, nor any personal possession of wives or children. . . . All such things were missing, but they had unlimited fruit off the trees and much other food which they did not get by agriculture, but the earth produced it of its own accord. They spent most of the time in the open air without clothes or bedding. The variations in the weather did them no harm, and they had soft couches, because abundant grass grew out of the ground.'[1]

It was not until the theory of evolution in the nineteenth century that this rose-tinted view of primitive life was seriously challenged by thinkers.[2] John Locke, for example, seemed to picture the 'state of nature', i.e. primitive existence, as characterized by peace, goodwill, and altruism. Rousseau's sentimental adulation of the 'noble savage'—man untrammelled by the constraints of civilization—won him a prize at the Academy of Dijon in 1750, when he wrote an essay on the theme 'Have the arts and sciences conferred benefits on mankind?' and answered the question with a resounding negative.

Lucretius' brief description is neither cynical nor sentimental, but realistic, describing a life that was tough and simple, but not without attractiveness. In at least two points it needs correction. It seems much more likely that primitive man consumed enormous quantities of meat and fish rather than contenting himself with a vegetarian diet of acorns and berries (lines 939–42). And his life was certainly not 'solitary', as line 961 suggests: man, from

---

[1] 271E–272B.
[2] A partial exception is Thomas Hobbes of Malmesbury (1588–1679), who had been much more cynical, and in a famous phrase described the life of man in the state of nature as 'solitary, nasty, brutish and short'.

the start, seems to have been a gregarious creature, living in the close-knit intimacy of the pack.

27. The Growth of Civilization

(V. 1011-23)

'Men began to use huts, clothes and fire, and to unite in permanent marriage. This meant a softening of the race, as fire made their bodies less able to endure cold, while family life softened their hearts. Next came agreements among neighbours not to hurt each other and to have compassion on women and children.'

Inde casas postquam ac pellis ignemque pararunt,
et mulier coniuncta viro concessit in unum

*

cognita sunt, prolemque ex se videre creatam,
tum genus humanum primum mollescere coepit.
ignis enim curavit ut alsia corpora frigus   1015
non ita iam possent caeli sub tegmine ferre,
et Venus imminuit viris puerique parentum
blanditiis facile ingenium fregere superbum.
tunc et amicitiem coeperunt iungere aventes
finitimi inter se nec laedere nec violari,   1020
et pueros commendarunt muliebreque saeclum,
vocibus et gestu cum balbe significarent
imbecillorum esse aequum misererier omnis.

The contrast with primitive man is pointed and explicit. Dwellings are built instead of roaming abroad, clothes and fire are used, above all the common life of family and tribe leads in the direction of an ordered society. The account is extremely compressed, yet, with some omissions which will be noted, agrees well enough with what we know of the development of civilization. Its emphasis on parental love and family life as a civilizing influence is interesting. Lucretius had already[1] observed that the weakness of the human babe, completely dependent as it is on its parents for food and protection, contrasts strongly with the young animal, which in many cases enters the world fully equipped for its life-task of hunting for food and struggling for existence. But this very helplessness is the most effective of childhood's 'winning ways' (*blanditiis* 1018), because it calls forth sustained tenderness and care from the parent. Lucretius is surely right in seeing the emergence of gentleness instead of brute force as what distinguishes civilization from barbarism. And this quality first grew in the human family.

Equally important for the growth of civilization, as Lucretius here emphasizes, was man's capacity to co-operate. Man never was, as Rousseau seemed to imagine, a 'noble savage' with an ideal individuality which he agreed to submerge in a 'Social Contract'. From the first he was strongly gregarious. 'They began to form friendship', says Lucretius (1019). Though the basis of the pact was, no doubt, largely utilitarian (Epicurus has the phrase 'not to harm or be harmed'), it enabled man to survive and civilization to arise.

This account must, naturally, be supplemented at some points. What Epicurus and Lucretius did not know was that man has behind him a long and gruelling process of evolution. Some would add that, in the depths of his being, he still bears the marks of the pre-human. Homo Sapiens—man as we know him—is probably little more than 50,000 years old, but behind him lie at least half a million years of development from animal through sub-human life. There was Australopithecus who ranged South Africa and used flints but not fire, and Pithecanthropus who tended fire but could not make it. Two things distinguished Homo Sapiens from these near-human relations: he invented the first standard machine-tool—a stone chisel for mass-producing spear-heads and similar necessities—and he practised art. Thus in Europe, for example, when the mists clear to give us our first glimpse of human society, about 20,000 B.C., we find hunting cultures with splendid paintings in Spain. At about the same time, on the Eurasian tundra, hunting

[1] V. 222 sqq. (extract no. 24).

bands were following the reindeer and digging semi-subterranean houses framed with bone and roofed with turf. And though man's goods might be few, he had a fertile imagination, which cou'd produce fine line-drawings of elephants and bulls.

Later, at about 10,000 B.C., animals began to be domesticated and wooden houses appeared. Afterwards came the Neolithic Revolution, with village settlements and the cultivation of crops. Man had begun to exploit the earth and to tap its resources. By 6000 we find a well-organized village life, and by 4000 large cities like Jericho, with as many as 3,000 inhabitants. Mankind had achieved civilization. His success was due largely to his intelligence, but also to his power to collaborate with his fellow-men.

28. The Origin of Language

(V. 1028–61)

'It was instinct (*natura*, 1028) which drove men to utter various sounds, and it was practical convenience (*utilitas*, 1029) which caused them to denote different objects by different names. So babies point before they can speak, being already aware of the purpose for which they are to use their faculties of speech. So calves butt before their horns are formed, cubs tussle with paws and jaws which only just exist, and birds attempt to fly with wings barely formed.

No man invented names for things and taught everyone else. Why should he alone have been able to speak when others were not, and whence could he have conceived the idea of speech unless those around him were speaking? And how could he have compelled the others to accept *his* names for things?

There is nothing surprising in the origin of language when we reflect that even dumb animals express their emotions in various cries.'

At varios linguae sonitus natura subegit
mittere et utilitas expressit nomina rerum,
non alia longe ratione atque ipsa videtur   1030

protrahere ad gestum pueros infantia linguae,
cum facit ut digito quae sint praesentia monstrent.
sentit enim vis quisque suas quoad possit abuti.
cornua nata prius vitulo quam frontibus exstent,
illis iratus petit atque infestus inurget.   1035
at catuli pantherarum scymnique leonum
unguibus ac pedibus iam tum morsuque repugnant,
vix etiam cum sunt dentes unguesque creati.
alituum porro genus alis omne videmus
fidere et a pinnis tremulum petere auxiliatum.   1040
proinde putare aliquem tum nomina distribuisse
rebus et inde homines didicisse vocabula prima,
desiperest.   nam cur hic posset cuncta notare
vocibus et varios sonitus emittere linguae,
tempore eodem alii facere id non quisse putentur? 1045
praeterea si non alii quoque vocibus usi
inter se fuerant, unde insita notities est
utilitatis et unde data est huic prima potestas,
quid vellet facere ut sciret animoque videret?
cogere item pluris unus victosque domare   1050
non poterat, rerum ut perdiscere nomina vellent.
nec ratione docere ulla suadereque surdis,
quid sit opus facto, facilest; neque enim paterentur
nec ratione ulla sibi ferrent amplius auris
vocis inauditos sonitus obtundere frustra.   1055
postremo quid in hac mirabile tantoperest re,
si genus humanum, cui vox et lingua vigeret,
pro vario sensu varia res voce notaret?
cum pecudes mutae, cum denique saecla ferarum
dissimilis soleant voces variasque ciere,   1060
cum metus aut dolor est et cum iam gaudia gliscunt.

1028–40. To utter sounds is a spontaneous, instinctive activity, according to Lucretius. As such, it is brought forth by the practical demands of life, e.g. the need to express inner emotion or to describe external events. This acute analysis of the origin of speech is certainly verified in the life-history of the individual human being. The new-born babe quickly associates its own cries with the desire for food, then for attention, and so on. The mother, too, quickly detects a variety in the sounds produced, though an unsympathetic ear may totally fail to appreciate these variations on a theme.

At the other end of the scale it is equally clear that the life of a community could not develop unless a pattern of similarity were established and sounds became signs. For this reason speech becomes a distinctive achievement of man, as several modern investigators have emphasized. Thus J. Z. Young asserts that *the* determinative mark of man is his capacity to communicate through speech and symbols.[1] And Dr. Norbert Wiener states: 'What does differentiate man from other animals in a way which leaves us not the slightest degree of doubt, is that he is a talking animal. The impulse to communicate with his fellow-beings is so strong that not even the double deprivation of blindness and deafness can completely obliterate it.'[2]

This is well said, but we would add that speech is not necessarily confined to communication, either in origin or in its developed form. It is possible to speak from sheer intensity of feeling, without having anything to communicate.

1041–61. It may seem a work of supererogation to disprove the theory that one man assigned names to things, then taught everyone else. But Lucretius is here joining an argument which had already been proceeding for several centuries among the Greek philosophers when he wrote. The one side held that speech came 'by nature' ($\phi\acute{v}\sigma\epsilon\iota$), the other 'by convention' ($\theta\acute{e}\sigma\epsilon\iota$). Epicurus took the first view: 'Names, too, were not at first deliberately given to things, but men's natures according to their

---

[1] *Doubt and Certainty in Science* (The Reith Lectures for 1950).
[2] *The Human Use of Human Beings*, p. 2.

different nationalities had their own peculiar feelings and received their peculiar impressions.'[1]

On the other side was Plato, who, in the dialogue *Cratylus*, describes a 'lawgiver' who gives names to things, composing them in such a way that they will bear a correct relation to the thing named. So in Genesis ii. 19–20 God brought the beasts of the field and the fowl of the air to Adam to see what he would call them: 'and whatsoever Adam called every living creature, that was the name thereof'.

These rival explanations persisted side by side as late as the end of the nineteenth century, when some scholars, e.g. W. Schmidt, were prepared to believe that the first language was given by God to the first men by sheer miracle. Significantly, Darwin accepted Epicurus' account.

Lucretius' own argument against the 'lawgiver' is threefold. First, why should one human being have this special faculty and no one else? (1043–5). Second, how could one man form the concept of what language was, without actual examples of talking people from which to derive it? (1046–9). Third, since he would be uttering sounds which were completely meaningless to those around, why should they take the slightest notice? (1050–5).

Then he comes to the real explanation: speech arises from the different sounds produced to correspond to different emotions, as is illustrated even in animal cries. This is surely on the right lines. We need to add that, behind even the most primitive forms of speech, there are many thousands of years of evolutionary development; and that the first framers of speech were probably very like babies—lively creatures who babbled and shouted and gave vent to their feelings vocally, and in so doing stumbled upon a medium for expressing their thoughts and desires—for communicating, in fact.

[1] *Ep. ad Her.* 75.

29. The Origin of Religion
(V. 1161–93)

'There are two reasons why belief in gods spread through the world, with such dire results:

'1. (1169–82) From early days men, both awake and asleep, had visions of divine figures of wonderful size and beauty. To these they attributed the power of sensation because they appeared to move their limbs and to utter appropriately dignified speech. Men credited them with immortality because they were ever-present and powerful, and with supreme happiness because they were free from the fear of death and able in visions and dreams to perform miracles.

'2. (1183–93) Men observed the orderly succession of celestial phenomena and the seasons, and attributed these to the divine will of the gods. They located the home of the gods in the sky because they saw the same natural processes of day and night, sun, moon, and stars occur in it; likewise snow, wind, and storm, which seemed like threats from the gods.'

Nunc quae causa deum per magnas numina gentis
pervulgarit et ararum compleverit urbis
suscipiendaque curarit sollemnia sacra,
quae nunc in magnis florent sacra rebu' locisque,
unde etiam nunc est mortalibus insitus horror   1165
qui delubra deum nova toto suscitat orbi
terrarum et festis cogit celebrare diebus,
non ita difficilest rationem reddere verbis.
quippe etenim iam tum divum mortalia saecla
egregias animo facies vigilante videbant   1170
et magis in somnis mirando corporis auctu.
his igitur sensum tribuebant propterea quod
membra movere videbantur vocesque superbas
mittere pro facie praeclara et viribus amplis.

aeternamque dabant vitam, quia semper eorum   1175
suppeditabatur facies et forma manebat,
et tamen omnino quod tantis viribus auctos
non temere ulla vi convinci posse putabant.
fortunisque ideo longe praestare putabant,
quod mortis timor haud quemquam vexaret eorum,   1180
et simul in somnis quia multa et mira videbant
efficere et nullum capere ipsos inde laborem.
praeterea caeli rationes ordine certo
et varia annorum cernebant tempora verti
nec poterant quibus id fieret cognoscere causis.   1185
ergo perfugium sibi habebant omnia divis
tradere et illorum nutu facere omnia flecti.
in caeloque deum sedis et templa locarunt,
per caelum volvi quia nox et luna videtur,
luna dies et nox et noctis signa severa   1190
noctivagaeque faces caeli flammaeque volantes,
nubila sol imbres nix venti fulmina grando
et rapidi fremitus et murmura magna minarum.

We should say that the second of Lucretius' reasons was much nearer the mark than the first. But for Lucretius himself the first is the correct explanation of the facts. For he has shown in Book IV that the basis of all knowledge is sensation; and the images of the gods received by men especially when asleep are the *simulacra* from the divine bodies: therefore the gods must exist. On the other hand, says Lucretius, the regularity in movement of the heavenly bodies, under which primitive man lived out his precarious existence, and the terrifying phenomena with which those bodies were linked, caused the doubly false inference that the world was under the government of divine beings who were capricious tyrants.

Religion seems to be a primary and universal experience of mankind; but its origin, unlike that of civilization and speech, is almost completely obscure. We content ourselves with mentioning two of the host of over-simplified explanations that have been offered. First is that of Statius, in the ancient world, who declared . *Primus in orbe deos fecit timor.*[1] The slight element of truth here is balanced by the fact that primitive religion, as anthropologists have discovered, contains joy as well as fear. Statius' aphorism is no more than a half-truth.

Second is the psycho-analytical explanation of Freud, who put forward a detailed account of how religion starts in the individual infant. In the infant mind the father inevitably stands for authority and the imposition of a strong will (whereas the mother means security, comfort, and pleasure). The father tends both to overawe and to fascinate the infant, who builds up a strong image of him as the all-powerful source of authority. This father-image becomes the concept of God. 'God', Freud concludes, 'is at bottom nothing more than an exalted father.'[2] This explanation too may have some truth, but it is rapidly becoming out of date, as the majority of fathers nowadays are much less authoritarian than when Freud put forward his theory.

Finally, if we turn from theories to factual evidence, we know that Neanderthal Man buried his dead, with food and weapons. Does this point to a cult of the dead as the beginning of religion? Or may Lucretius' second reason be the right one, since both Stone Age hunters and Australian bushmen have myths of the sun and sky as objects of reverence? Miss Jacquetta Hawkes makes out a strong case for the sun as among the prime objects of worship: 'In the dawn of mind, sunrise and sunset, if not the sun itself, seem likely to have been among the first things to have been named by the first man. . . . A kind of awe may have been felt even by the earliest man for this unreachable, eye-dazzling presence in the skies.'[3]

[1] *Theb.* 3. 661.
[2] *The Future of an Illusion*, p. 76.
[3] *Man and the Sun*, p. 46.

30. True Piety

(V. 1194–1203)

'What folly it was for man to attribute anger and interference to the gods, thus causing sorrow for themselves, for us, and for future generations! True piety consists, not in the frequent and meticulous performance of superstitious rites, but in the power to contemplate the universe with a mind at peace.'

Lucretius shows close acquaintance with the details of Roman ritual which he so strongly condemns. The Roman prayed with his head covered (*velatum*, 1198), the Greek with it bare. The worshipper approached with the statue of the god on his right hand; after praying, he turned to face it (*vertier ad lapidem*, 1199). After facing the statue, he prostrated himself in an attitude of worship (*procumbere humi prostratum*, 1200). Spreading, not clasping, the hands was the Roman attitude of prayer (*pandere palmas*, 1200).

O genus infelix humanum, talia divis
cum tribuit facta atque iras adiunxit acerbas!   1195
quantos tum gemitus ipsi sibi, quantaque nobis
vulnera, quas lacrimas peperere minoribu' nostris!
nec pietas ullast velatum saepe videri
vertier ad lapidem atque omnis accedere ad aras
nec procumbere humi prostratum et pandere palmas 1290
ante deum delubra nec aras sanguine multo
spargere quadrupedum nec votis nectere vota,
sed mage pacata posse omnia mente tueri.

According to Bailey,[1] Epicurus did not condemn the worship of the gods, and in the treatise on 'Piety' says: 'Let us sacrifice piously and rightly, where it is customary, and let us do all things righteously according to the laws, not troubling ourselves with common beliefs in what concerns the noblest and holiest beings.'

[1] Commentary, pp. 1513–14.

'or Epicurus it is not the act of worship which is wrong, but the
alse belief about the gods. True piety is 'to have no fear of god
nd to cease from anxiety'.[1] Lucretius says the same in 1203.

If Bailey is right, Epicurus and Lucretius can be said to have
rasped something of what true religion is about. It is about the
sacred', that which evokes both awe and attraction. At its lowest
he sacred is symbolized in crude totem and fetish, explained in
antastic myth, and propitiated by bloodthirsty sacrifice. At its
ighest, if saints and mystics are not deluded, it is a serene sense
f intimate unity with the source of all beauty, truth, and goodness,
which purifies the consciousness and leads to solid ethical achieve-
nent.

Perhaps indeed religious experience is the culmination of the
whole evolutionary process and the clue to its meaning.

[1] Plutarch, *Contr. Ep. Beat.* 8. 1092b.

BOOK VI

In Book V Lucretius has argued that science, in the shape of the atomic theory of Epicurus, can account for all the regular features of the universe including the origin of our world and the growth of human society. But what of its irregular features? Even if divine intervention is inexorably ruled out of normal events and experiences, is there not a place left for religion in the abnormal, the mysterious, the inexplicable? Lucretius' last task is to expose and destroy even this refuge by offering a scientific account of such abnormal occurrences as thunder and lightning, thunderbolts,[1] waterspouts, earthquakes, and volcanic eruptions, which seem supernatural, but are susceptible of a purely natural explanation.

It would be fairly generally agreed that any religion which depends for its acceptance on the spectacular and the inexplicable is doomed today by the onward march of science. To this extent Lucretius' position seems part of our climate of thought. Like him, we are disinclined to believe that a realm of arbitrary and chaotic magic can coexist with that world of scientific investigation in which evidence is carefully collected and weighed in order to gain a reasoned interpretation of the facts and an accurate prediction of the effects which follow causes. Nevertheless, from Lucretius' time to our own century, men have persisted in explaining the unusual and the catastrophic by miracle and magic. As recently as Shakespeare's day it was generally believed that frogs and lemmings were spontaneously generated in the clouds, that witches transported themselves on wings if not on broomsticks, and that the devil frequently appeared in the shape of a black boy.

Whatever then may be said for Lucretius' general philosophy, he is surely right in this book to decry the attempt to find room for religion in the gaps left over from scientific discovery. Per-

[1] The Romans distinguished between *fulgur*, the lightning-flash seen in the sky, and *fulmen*, the 'thunderbolt'—i.e. the lightning-stroke which descended to earth. Greek too has different words for these.

haps he has made even sharper the choice that has faced men since the scientific discoveries of the nineteenth century, as Charles Kingsley saw: 'They find now that they have got rid of an inte-- fering God—a master magician, as I call it—they have to choose between the absolute empire of accident, and the living, immanent, ever-working God.'[1]

31. Thunderbolts

(VI. 379–99)

'The way to understand the thunderbolt is not to consult Etruscan scrolls in search of the hidden purposes of the gods, marking whence it came and whither it goes, how its blow pierces barriers and pollutes the spot where it strikes. But if the gods are respon- sible, why do they not cause the guilty to be struck instead of the innocent? And why do they attack desert places? Are they prac- tising? Then why do they waste the bolt and blunt it against the ground?'

Lucretius' treatment of thunderbolts is very full, and occupies lines 219–422. He first gives the 'scientific' explanation (219–378), and to this *hoc* in line 379 refers. Then he refutes the popular belief that the thunderbolt is the instrument of divine vengeance, and our extract is the first part of this refutation.

Hoc est igniferi naturam fulminis ipsam
perspicere et qua vi faciat rem quamque videre,   380
non Tyrrhena retro volventem carmina frustra
indicia occultae divum perquirere mentis,
unde volans ignis pervenerit aut in utram se
verterit hinc partim, quo pacto per loca saepta
insinuarit, et hinc dominatus ut extulerit se,   385
quidve nocere queat de caelo fulminis ictus.
quod si Iuppiter atque alii fulgentia divi

[1] C. Kingsley, *Life*, quoted by C. E. Raven, *Science, Religion and the Future*, p. 33.

terrifico quatiunt sonitu caelestia templa
et iaciunt ignem quo cuiquest cumque voluntas,
cur quibus incautum scelus aversabile cumquest   39c
non faciunt icti flammas ut fulguris halent
pectore perfixo, documen mortalibus acre,
et potius nulla sibi turpi conscius in re
volvitur in flammis innoxius inque peditur
turbine caelesti subito correptus et igni?   395
cur etiam loca sola petunt frustraque laborant?
an tum bracchia consuescunt firmantque lacertos?
in terraque patris cur telum perpetiuntur
obtundi? cur ipse sinit neque parcit in hostis?

379–86. In choosing the thunderbolt for scientific explanation, Lucretius is shrewdly challenging one of the most spectacular and, at the same time, superstitious aspects of Roman religion. For the lightning-stroke was not only the traditional weapon of the gods for punishing offenders, but the means by which they declared their will to man, if he could divine it.

The systematic development of divination—i.e. the discovery of the will of the gods through signs and portents—came to Roman religion from the Etruscans, who had highly developed methods both of interpreting the signs of nature, and also of extracting omens from such repulsively surgical methods as the minute examination of the victim's liver. The practical Roman, though far more devoted to this world than the next, was nevertheless extremely superstitious. He used omens not so much to foretell the future as to find out what it was most expedient to do in the present. Should the farmer sow his field, or the general offer battle, at that precise time? These were questions to be interpreted by omens.

But what constituted an omen? Almost any happening of an unusual nature, even a sneeze or a stumble. A more important question was who decided what the omen meant. Any prominent person was considered competent to observe omens, e.g. a pater-

amilias, a magistrate, or a general in the field. But the decision
whether they were good or bad needed the special skill of the
augur. His verdict, astonishingly enough, was accepted without
question; and this fact was sometimes turned to advantage by
unscrupulous politicians and obliging augurs. Rome's public
business was on more than one important occasion completely
held up by the simple announcement in the Senate that an official
was about to watch the heavens. Two well-known instances of this
have already been mentioned.[1]

At the time of Lucretius State religion was in decay. Yet, such
was the power of superstition over the Roman that Cicero and his
fellow-senators spent much time in January 56 B.C. considering
whether a quotation from the Sibylline Books should prevent the
Roman army from going to Egypt. On the opposite side, however,
may be quoted the action of a Roman admiral in the First Punic
War. The sacred chickens (birds which were taken round in coops
on military campaigns; if they ate greedily, the omen was good; if
they showed distaste, it was bad) went off their food during a
campaign. Accordingly, he ordered them to be thrown into the
sea with the words: 'If they will not eat, let them drink.' In the
ensuing engagement he lost nearly all his ships, and the incident
circulated widely as a cautionary tale.

390–95. Why must the innocent suffer? The question must
surely be as old as the human race itself. The attempt to justify
the ways of God (or gods) to men has engaged the attention not
only of philosophers and theologians, but also of poets and ordinary men. In Homer's *Odyssey* Philoetius complains: 'Father Zeus,
what a cruel god you are! There is none harder. In dealing out
misfortunes, misery, and suffering to us men, no sense of mercy
holds you back; yet it was you who caused us to be born.'[2] The
resolution of this dilemma (called 'theodicy' by philosophers) was
attempted by Aeschylus in his *Prometheus Bound*, and by the
author of Job in the Old Testament. Both achieved a magnificent
poem which drew attention to the problem and challenged the
prevailing orthodoxy, but reached no real solution. Plato faced it

[1] See commentary on Book I, p. 3.
[2] XX. 201–3 in E. V. Rieu's translation (Penguin).

in the *Republic*, and in the Myth of Er[1] put forward a system of rewards and punishments after death, together with the necessity for endless rebirths, as a solution to the problem of innocent suffering.

This solution closely resembled those of the Indian religions, Hinduism and Buddhism. Both these religions accept the fact of human suffering which seems arbitrary, yet insist that the universe is ethically sound. The rigid law of cause and effect, Karma, runs throughout the universe, and a man's destiny in this life is linked directly to the accumulated debits and credits of countless previous existences. Thus, whatever happens to him must be thoroughly deserved. Yet Hindus must hesitate to apply this theory to their own great leader, Gandhi, who, after a life of such devotion that he was widely hailed as a 'Mahatma' (i.e. special manifestation of God), died at the hand of a fanatical gunman.

On the Epicurean hypothesis, that the universe is the product of blind forces, a theodicy is unnecessary. But if it has a purpose, connected with a divine being who governs it, the problem posed by Lucretius' sardonic question is acute. We leave aside the theologians, whose contributions are too numerous to mention, and single out one voice from the other side, to which Lucretius might have been willing to listen—that of Albert Einstein, who said: 'The God who creates and is nature is very difficult to understand, but he is not arbitrary or malicious.'[2] The physical laws of the universe are inexorable. There are no special exemptions, and God allows his thunderbolt, like the rain, to fall on both the just and the unjust. Yet there is a constancy about the universe which never deceives, and in this lies our hope. If it is not a carefully protected nursery, neither is it a bedlam of anarchic confusion.

[1] *Rep.* X. 614 sqq.
[2] Quoted by H. E. Huntley, *The Faith of a Physicist*, p. 70.

32. The True Explanation of Volcanic Eruption

(VI. 680–702)

'The reason why the flame is ignited and bursts from the furnace of Etna is this. The mountain is hollow and supported on rocky caverns, in which there is air and wind. When the wind has become hot, it heats the surrounding rocks and earth, and strikes fire from them. Then it rises and bursts forth from the crater, hurling out ashes, smoke, and great boulders. Also, from the sea which is constantly dashing against the foot of the mountain, a mixture of wind and water enters and spouts up to the summit, shooting forth flames, rocks, and sand.'

Nunc tamen illa modis quibus irritata repente   680
flamma foras vastis Aetnae fornacibus efflet,
expediam.   primum totius subcava montis
est natura, fere silicum suffulta cavernis.
omnibus est porro in speluncis ventus et aer.
ventus enim fit, ubi est agitando percitus, aer.   685
hic ubi percaluit calefecitque omnia circum
saxa furens, qua contingit, terramque, et ab ollis
excussit calidum flammis velocibus ignem,
tollit se ac rectis ita faucibus eicit alte.
fert itaque ardorem longe longeque favillam   690
differt et crassa volvit caligine fumum
extruditque simul mirando pondere saxa;
ne dubites quin haec animai turbida sit vis.
praeterea magna ex parti mare montis ad eius
radices frangit fluctus aestumque resorbet.   695
ex hoc usque mari speluncae montis ad altas

perveniunt subter fauces.   hac ire fatendumst

*

et penetrare mari penitus res cogit aperto
atque efflare foras ideoque extollere flammam
saxaque subiectare et harenae tollere nimbos.   700
in summo sunt vertice enim crateres, ut ipsi
nominitant, nos quod fauces perhibemus et ora.

Volcanic eruptions would clearly be a fruitful source of superstitious fear, both because their physical explanation was unknown
and also because Etna's eruptions were frequent and damaging.
Lucretius has already referred to them,[1] and Cicero mentions
the destruction of Catana in 122 B.C.[2] Better known to us is the
eruption of Vesuvius over a hundred years later, in A.D. 79, which
destroyed the cities of Pompeii and Herculaneum. Of this we
have an eyewitness account by Pliny the Younger, in two letters[3]
written to the historian Tacitus; but prior to this Vesuvius had
long been quiescent. The last big eruption of Vesuvius occurred
in March 1944, when a stream of lava, half a mile wide, flowed
down its slopes to the coastal plain, destroying the little town of
San Sebastiano. Etna, by contrast, is now quiescent.

Lucretius' attempt at an explanation is credible and twofold.
First he develops the concept of hot air in motion, which melts
the earth and rocks, then forces them through the narrow opening
of the crater. But this is insufficient to account for the other
material which is thrust out—sand, for example. So he suggests
that sea-water must also enter. This is feasible, since all volcanoes
known to the Romans were near the sea, and it is at least possible
to imagine sea-water draining through the subsoil. The actual
explanation of volcanic activity is that, beneath the earth's solid
outer crust, rock material exists at immensely high temperatures
and pressure. When this pressure is relieved locally, the rock
material becomes fluid, and rises to the surface through the paths
of least resistance. Where the earth's crust is unstable, an opening

[1] II. 593 (extract no. 13).
[2] *De Nat. Deorum* II. 38.   [3] *Ep.* VI. 16 and 20.

is produced, through which this material is forced in eruption. The masses of steam which are so much a part of volcanic eruptions may partially derive from crater lakes, or in some cases, as Lucretius suggests, from the sea, but also, most probably, from the rock material itself.

So ends our selection from Lucretius' attempt to 'seek out the causes of things', to set forth a rational and purely natural explanation of all phenomena. He has shown that the explanation of physical events must be in physical terms, and, in so doing, he has discarded all merely superstitious supernaturalism. He has not destroyed religion. But he has shown that, if a particular religion fails to give an adequate vision of reality through its symbols, then reality is best affirmed by denying that particular form of religion. Lucretius' own vision is too narrow, partial, and dogmatic to form an acceptable frame of reference for men today. But to convince us of the necessity for such a vision—a vision which will reconcile man to the universe and to his own being—is perhaps the greatest achievement of his disciplined but kindling imagination.

NOTES

1. Invocation to Venus, the Creative Power of Nature
(I. 1–25)

1. **Aeneadum,** gen. plur. of *Aeneades*, 1st decl. noun with Greek form of the nom. sing. The ending *-um* as a 1st decl. gen. plur. is found only in (i) nouns borrowed from Greek, (ii) (in verse only) native Latin words ending in *-cola* and *-gena*. The myth that the Romans were 'the descendants of Aeneas', soon to be enshrined in Vergil's *Aeneid*, had already appeared in Naevius' epic poem on the First Punic War. **divum,** gen. plur. of *divus*, of which *dius* (22) is another form. The root *di-* means 'gleam'; from the idea of 'brightness' (cf. *dies*) develops that of 'divinity' (cf. *deus, Dis, Diana*, etc.). The form *dius* is always an adj. meaning (i) rarely 'bright', (ii) 'divine'; the form *divus* is rare as an adj., but common as a noun in all genders: *divus = deus* (as here), *diva = dea* (12), *divum = caelum* in the phrase *sub divo*. The ending *-um* was the original gen. plur. of 2nd decl. nouns and adjs. Later the pronoun ending *-orum* gradually spread first to adjs., then to nouns. As a noun-ending it was still regarded as a new fashion by Cicero, who would allow either *deorum* or *deum*, but only *triumvirum, sestertium, nummum.*

2. **alma,** 'life-giving', connected with *alo*, 'foster', 'nourish'; a traditional epithet of Venus in Roman poets, here especially appropriate to Venus as the 'life-force' behind Nature. **signa** usually refers to stars or constellations in Lucr., but here is used in a wider sense, equivalent to *sidera*, to mean 'heavenly bodies' including the sun and moon.

3. **navigerum, frugiferentis:** see 'Language', p. xxvi and 'Metre', p. xxxiii.

4. **concelebras,** 'fill with your presence'. The primary idea is of a crowd thronging: so in II. 345 (extract no. 12) of a flock of birds. **animantum:** *-um* for *-ium* in the gen. plur. for words ending in *-ns* is a licence not uncommon in Lucr. and other poets, *-ium* following a long syllable being almost impossible in a hexameter. In origin

animans has a wider meaning than *animal* and includes all that lives—men, beasts, and plants—though it is commonly used in the more restricted sense of *animal*.

5. **visitque exortum.** The logical order would be *exortumque visit; exortum*, 'having risen up', agrees with *genus*.

6. **te . . . te . . . te . . . tibi . . . tibi.** Note the powerful repetition. Miss Brophy compares the *Gloria in Excelsis: Laudamus te, Benedicimus te, Adoramus te*, etc. **fugiunt :** the winds flee from Venus because she brings peace and calm.

7. **adventumque tuum** amplifies *te*; so in 12–13 *te . . . tuumque . . . initum*. **tibi,** 'for you', i.e. 'at your bidding'. **suavīs,** acc. plur.; see 'Metre', p. xxxi. **daedala tellus,** 'the ingenious earth' or 'earth, the artificer' (Bailey). The adj. may also have the passive meaning 'cunningly wrought'. The Eng. 'daedal' is used in the active sense by Spenser in his adaptation of the present passage, in the passive sense by Shelley, *Prometheus Unbound* IV. 415–17 :

> Language is a perpetual Orphic song,
> Which rules with Daedal harmony a throng
> Of thoughts and shapes, which else senseless and shapeless were.

8. **summittit,** 'brings forth'. **rident :** cf. Catullus, LXIV. 274, (*undae*) *leviter sonant plangore cachinni*. **aequora,** 'levels': *aequor* (from *aequus*) means a flat, level surface, and is most frequently used of the surface of the sea, but also of a plain, e.g. III. 1002 (extract no. 19).

9. **placatum,** 'having been appeased', i.e. after the storm.

10. **species . . . verna diei :** see 'Style', p. xxv. **patĕfactast =** *patefacta est*. Prodelision (as Eng. *he 's*), not elision (as French *j'ai*), takes place in Latin when *es* or *est* follows a word ending in a vowel or *-m*, and was at this period often, though not always, written as it was pronounced. The *e* of *patefacio* and *patefio*, originally long, was often shortened for metrical convenience.

11. 'and the fertilizing breath of Zephyr having been unbarred is blowing fresh'. **reserata :** see p. 10. **genitabilis :** a rare word, used here *metri gratia* for the more usual *genitalis*, which occurs in I. 58 (extract no. 2).

12. **aeriae :** see n. on *aer* VI. 684 (extract no. 32). **primum.** The birds are the first to feel the coming of spring, before the animals: so Verg. *Georgics* II. 328, Ovid, *Fasti* IV. 99, Chaucer, *Prologue* I. 11, 'So priketh hem nature in hir corages'.

13. **perculsae corda,** 'their hearts thrilled', lit. 'thrilled as to their hearts'; *corda* acc. of respect or part affected: cf. Verg. *Georgics* IV. 357 *percussa nova mentem formidine,* 'her mind stricken with a new dread'. **tua vi :** see 'Metre', p. xxxii.

14. **inde,** 'next', following *primum* (12). **ferae pecudes,** 'wild beasts and cattle'. The collocation of two words of similar meaning without a conjunction was common in archaic and legal Latin (e.g. *pugnant proeliant*, Ennius ap. Non. 472. 31; *aequum bonum*, Cic. *Topica* 17). With two words of contrasted meaning and with three or more words, asyndeton is the normal rule in all periods and types of composition. **laeta,** 'rich'. Vergil begins the *Georgics* with the words *Quid faciat laetas segetes . . . .*

15. **ita** = *adeo*: 'so captivated by delight, each eagerly follows you wherever you go on leading it'; *capta* agrees with *quaeque* understood (from *quamque* in the *quo* clause) as the subject of *sequitur*. **lepore** here is the subjective feeling of delight, almost *voluptate*; normally it means objective beauty or charm, as in I. 934 (extract no. 7).

17. **denique** follows *primum* (12) and *inde* (14): first birds, then beasts and cattle, then all things are gripped by the power of Venus.

19. **omnibus** etc., 'instilling into' or 'inspiring in the breasts of all'. With parts of the body in Latin the possessor is expressed as the indirect object of the verb rather than as a gen. or possessive adj. qualifying the noun: cf. French, *je me suis coupé le doigt*. **incutiens.** The word is more often used of inspiring fear, but is used of love again in I. 924 (extract no. 7).

20. **saecla,** 'races', 'breeds': see 'Metre', p. xxx.

21. **quae quoniam,** '(and) since you . . .'; *quae* is the co-ordinating relative, here equivalent to *et . . . tu*, though the 'and' may well be omitted in tr. **rerum naturam :** see Introduction, p. xi. **gubernas :** Venus 'guides' Nature because love is the cause of creation for all that lives.

22. **dīas,** see note on *divum* (1); here more probably 'bright' than

'divine'. **luminis oras,** 'the realms of light', i.e. the world; *ora* properly means 'border', hence the plural comes to mean 'region' (cf. *finis* and *fines*).

24. **te . . . studeo . . . esse,** 'I desire you to be'; *studeo* most often governs a dat. and means 'am zealous for', but the present meaning and construction are quite common in prose. **scribendis versibus,** dat. of purpose with *sociam*, lit. 'partner for . . .', but tr. 'in'.

25. **pangere,** 'to compose'.

2. Exhortation to the Reader: the Origin of Matter (I. 50–61)

50. **quod superest,** 'next', 'to continue', a stock phrase by which Lucr. indicates transition to another topic; lit. '(as for that) which remains', the antecedent to *quod* being an understood *id,* acc. of respect. **sagacem,** 'keen', 'shrewd', the predominant significance of the word; primarily it means 'keen-scented' of hounds etc.

51. **semotum a curis.** This freedom from cares is the exact equivalent of *ataraxia,* the Epicurean ideal (see Introduction, p. xiv). **rationem.** The main uses of *ratio* in Lucr. are: (i) 'thinking', 'reasoning', 'reason' (I. 935, II. 82, 94); (ii) 'theory', 'system of philosophy', 'doctrine' (I. 51, 81, 943, 946); (iii) 'account', especially in the phrase *rationem reddo,* 'render an account' (I. 59); (iv) 'system', 'workings', 'law' (I. 54, 148); (v) in the abl. sing. (like *modo* and *pacto*), 'way', 'manner', 'means' (I. 77, 153, 280, 948).

52. **disposta,** see 'Metre', p. xxx. **fideli,** abl. with *studio,* 'with loyal zeal'.

53. **intellecta . . . sint:** subjunctive because the clause is virtually sub-oblique, depending on a purpose clause; the writer's thought is *'ne mea dona contempta relinquat, prius quam intellecta erunt'.* **contempta relinquas,** 'scorn and reject'.

54. **summa . . . ratione,** 'supreme law', or possibly *summa* is transferred epithet, 'the workings of the heavens on high' (Bailey). See note on *rationem* (51).

55. **rerum primordia,** 'first-beginnings of things', Lucretius' distinctive expression for 'atoms'. His most frequent synonyms occur in 58 and 59: *corpora,* 'particles' (which he uses with or

without the adj. *genitalia*), and *semina*, 'seeds' (with or without *rerum*). Note that *primordia* is the antecedent to the three relative clauses introduced by *unde* (56), *quo* (57), and *quae* (58).

56. **unde,** 'from which, as I shall show'. Of the three relative clauses qualifying *primordia*, the first two have subjunctive, the third indicative: the *unde* and *quo* clauses are virtually sub-oblique— i.e. Lucr. is not yet stating as an agreed fact that nature creates all things from atoms, but quoting the doctrine he is setting out to prove. **creet . . . auctet,** asyndeton; see note on *ferae pecudes* I. 14 (extract no. 1).

57. **quove,** 'and into which'; *quoque* is avoided either for reasons of euphony or in case it should be confused with a part of *quisque*; so also IV. 28 (extract no. 20) and so Verg. *Aen.* II. 102, IX. 376, 377, XII. 313. **eadem . . . perempta,** 'the same things when destroyed', referring to *omnis res* in the previous line; Lucr. not infrequently picks up *res* with a neuter or vice versa. **rursum :** an older form of *rursus*, not uncommon in Cicero; see 'Language', p. xxvii.

58. **materiem.** Lucr. varies between *materia* (1) and *materies* (5) in the nom. and acc. sing.; in other cases only *materia* is used. **genitalia corpora rebus** = *rerum primordia* (55 n.). Although grammatically *rebus* must be construed with the adj. (lit. 'creative for things'), in sense it is equivalent to a gen. with *corpora*; similarly such a dative as *omnibus* I. 19 (extract no. 1) has the meaning of a gen. with the noun denoting a part of the body, though its grammatical construction is indirect object of the verb.

59. **reddunda in ratione,** 'in rendering my account', a mercantile metaphor; see n. on *rationem* (51). Note the older form of the 3rd conj. gerundive in *-undus*: see 'Language', p. xxvii. **semina rerum** = *rerum primordia* (55 n.).

60. **suemus :** contracted for *suevimus*, perfect of *suesco* used in a present sense, 'we are (lit. have become) accustomed'. See also 'Metre', p. xxxi. **usurpare :** notice (*a*) the 5th foot spondee, (*b*) the quadrisyllabic ending: see 'Metre', p. xxxiii.

3. Religion Overthrown by Philosophy (I. 62–79)

62. **ante oculos foede . . . iaceret in terris,** 'lay for all to see foully grovelling upon the ground' (Rouse).

63. **religione.** See Lewis & Short for the different senses of *religio*; here the meaning is 'religion', as it is in I. 78, 83, 101, and, in the plur. form, 932. See also 'Metre', pp. xxix and xxxiii.

64. **a caeli regionibus,** 'from the quarters of the sky', because the sky was supposed to be the abode of the gods. **ostendebat:** cf. *usurpare* I. 60 n. (extract no. 2). Lucr. tends to reinforce an unusual metrical or grammatical usage with two or more instances close together.

65. **super:** adv. = *desuper*, 'from above'.

66. **primum:** adv. with *tollere*, giving a slightly different sense from the adj. *primus* in the next line: 'a man of Greece dared for the first time to raise . . . and to be the first to stand in the way . . .'. **Graius homo:** Lucr. clearly means Epicurus, who, though not the first Greek to establish a physical theory of the universe, was the first to use a physical theory in order to refute religious views. See also 'Metre', p. xxix.

68. **deum:** objective gen., 'talk of (i.e. about) the gods'. For the gen. plur. ending -*um* see the n. on *divum* I. 1.

69. Note the clash of ictus and word-accent in the 5th foot, *èó màgis ăcrem*: see 'Metre', p. xxxii. Here again the rhythm produces an effect of excitement, but intellectual rather than physical.

70. **irritāt:** a very unusual contraction of *irritavit*: see 'Language', p. xxvii.

71. **cupiret** = *cuperet*: see 'Language', p. xxvii. There is no other instance in Latin of *cupio* treated as a 4th conj. verb. Note again the 'reinforcement': two exceptional grammatical forms occur in successive lines. Note also the alliteration and assonance in this and the next three lines: see 'Style', p. xxiv.

72. **extra:** prep. governing *moenia*.

73. **longe:** with *extra*, 'far beyond'. **flammantia moenia mundi,** 'the flaming walls of the world'. The lightest particles flew out to the edge of the *mundus* (see Introduction, p. xvi, n. 2), and in whirling round caught fire, forming an envelope of flame (*aether*).

74. **omne immensum,** 'the measureless universe'. Lucr. uses *omne* as a noun to denote the entire universe, consisting of countless

mundi. So Plato uses τὸ πᾶν, e.g. *Timaeus* 28 c. **peragravit**: *pe-răgra-vit*: see 'Metre', p. xxx.

75. **refert,** either 'brings back word' or (with Rouse, who remarks that *refert* keeps up the military metaphor and compares Verg. *Aen.* IV. 93 *spolia ampla refertis*) 'brings back his prize, the knowledge . . .' The objects of *refert* are three reported questions: (i) *quid possit oriri,* (ii) *quid nequeat* (sc. *oriri*), (iii) the rest of the sentence from *finita* to *haerens,* which should be construed thus: *denique* ('in other words') *quanam ratione* ('by what means', 'how') *cuique sit* ('each thing has') *finita potestas* ('limited power', i.e. 'a limit set to its power') *atque alte terminus haerens* ('and a deeply-fixed boundary-stone'): i.e. everything obeys natural laws; man need no longer fear the illimitable and the supernatural.

78. **pedibus subiecta.** Vergil echoes these words in *Georg.* II. 492: see Introduction, p. xiii.

79. **caelo:** dat. With *exaequo,* 'make equal to', 'place on a level with', Sallust and Livy, like Lucr., use dat., Cicero and Caesar use **cum.**

4. Iphigenia at Aulis (I. 80–101)

80. **illud** refers forward to the *ne*-clause: tr. 'One thing I fear in these matters is that . . .'.

81. **impia . . . rationis . . . elementa:** see 'Style', p. xxv; *ratio* = 'system of philosophy' as in I. 51 (extract no. 2). The objection that science is 'impious' has frequently been made. At the height of the Darwinian controversy a lady confided to a famous preacher, 'I do hope that Mr. Darwin will be proved wrong, or, if he is right, that the facts will not be widely known.' To his credit the preacher replied, 'Madam, the facts are God's facts, whatever they turn out to be.'

82. **indugredi:** see 'Language', p. xxvii. For the prefix *indu-* look up *indoles, industrius, indutiae* in Lewis & Short. **quod contra,** 'whereas on the contrary': *quod* acc. of respect (lit. 'as to which'); *contra* adv. **illa:** singling out *religio* as a target for his scorn, like Churchill's famous '*that* man' applied to Hitler.

83. **peperit,** 'has brought about', from *pario.*

84. **Aulide**: locative; take *quo pacto* first. **quo pacto**, 'as', 'for instance' (lit. 'in the way in which'); *pactum*, 'agreement', 'bargain', can in the abl. sing., like *modo* and *ratione*, also mean 'way', 'manner'. **Triviai**, 'of Artemis'. The appellation *Trivia* ('goddess of the crossways') really belongs not to the Greek Artemis, but to the Roman Diana, to whom altars were often set up at crossroads in Italy. For the form of the gen. sing. see 'Language', p. xxvii.

85. **Iphianassai**: note again the reinforcement by repetition of the archaic grammatical form. In Homer Iphianassa is the name of Agamemnon's youngest daughter, but Lucr. uses it as an alternative form of Iphigenia.

86. **prima virorum** = *primi viri*, 'the foremost heroes'. This use of neut. plur. adj. with dependent gen. is a Greek figure of speech which Lucr. commonly imitates: Ovid echoes the present phrase in *summa ducum Atrides* (*Amores* I. 9. 37).

87. **cui**, 'her (tresses)': see n. on *omnibus* I. 19 (extract no. 1). **simul** = *simul atque*. **infula**. Lucr. uses Roman terminology: the *infula* was a heavy band of twisted wool worn round the head by priests and priestesses, and also placed on the heads of sacrificial animals. The ends of the strands were left hanging down on either side. I. realizes the truth as soon as the *infula* is placed on her head instead of the *vitta*, the simple hairband worn by a bride. **comptūs** here = *cŏmas*, which would not scan; *comptus* is not connected with *coma*, but is derived from *como*: see n. on *compta* I. 950 (extract no. 7). See also 'Language', p. xxvi. The acc. is governed by the prefix in *circumdatus*, 'placed round . . .'; the dat. is normal, e.g. Lucr. VI. 1035–6 *aer omnibus est rebus circumdatus*.

88. **ex utraque pari . . . parte**, 'in equal lengths on both sides': a combination of *ex utraque parte*, 'on both sides', and *utraque parte pari*, 'with both sides equal'. N.B. *ūt-ra-que*: see *Metre*, p. xxx. **malarum**, 'of her cheeks'; *mala* strictly means 'cheekbone', but is often used in verse in place of *gena*, the normal word for 'cheek'. **profusast**, middle voice, 'hung down'; see also n. on *patefactast* I. 10 (extract no. 1).

89. **simul** repeats the *simul* of 87.

90. **hunc propter**, 'beside him'; 'near' is the primary meaning of *propter*, formed from *prope* as *subter* from *sub*.

91. **aspectu . . . suo**, 'at the sight of her'; the possessive adj. has the force of an objective gen.

92. **summissa**, middle, 'sinking'.

93. **in tali tempore**: *tempus* is here almost a synonym for *periculum*, and so has a 'place where' rather than a 'time when' construction: cf. Cic. *Pro Quinct.* 1, *in hoc tempore*. **quibat**: from *queo*, conjugated like *eo*; the subject is the *quod* clause of the next line, 'nor could it avail . . . that . . .'

94. **princeps** = *prima*: 'she had been the first to give the name of father to the king'. So in Euripides (*Iph. Aul.* 1220) I., begging for her life, says to her father: ''Twas I first called thee father, thou me child' (tr. A. S. Way).

95. **sublata**: perfect participle of *tollo*. See 'Metre', p. xxx.

96. **sollemni**, 'customary', 'traditional'; the root meaning of the word is 'annual'.

97. **claro**, 'loud'. **comitari**, 'to be escorted': not from the deponent *comitor*, but from *comito*, an active verb with the same meaning, rare and poetic except for the perfect particle passive *comitatus*, 'accompanied', which is common in prose. **Hymenaeo**, 'wedding song'. At a Roman wedding the words *Hymen, o Hymenaee* were shouted: so Catullus LXI and LXII.

98. **casta inceste . . . hostia concideret**, 'fall a sinless victim to a sinful rite' (Latham). The pathos is heightened by the antithesis of *casta inceste* and the alliteration of *mactatu maesta*.

99. **mactatu**: see 'Language', p. xxvi. **parentis**: subjective gen., 'a father's slaying' (of his daughter).

101. **tantum . . . malorum**: we should normally expect this phrase to be, as in V. 227 (extract no. 24) it is, a poetic variant for *tot mala*; but here, clearly, the meaning is rather 'such depths of wickedness'. **suadere** with acc. means 'prompt', 'suggest'. More often a reported statement or command—or even question, as in V. 1053 (extract no. 28)—takes the place of the acc., and the person to whom the suggestion is made appears in the dat.; thus the verb comes to mean 'urge', 'advise'.

5. 'Nothing can be Created out of Nothing' (I. 146–66)

146. necessest . . . discutiant (148), 'must dispel'; *discutiant* semi-dependent jussive subjunctive. In tr. it will be best to turn this sentence into the passive to preserve the Latin word-order: 'this terror . . . must be dispelled, not by the rays of the sun' etc.

147. tela, 'shafts'.

148. species ratioque, 'outward form and inward law'; *ratio* as in I. 54 (extract no. 2).

149. Rouse tr. 'and her first principle we will derive from this' (lit. 'whose first-principle will for us take its beginning hence'); *cuius* refers to *naturae* in the previous line; *nobis* is ethic dat., denoting the person interested in the action of the verb, cf. Hor. *Sat.* I. 9. 4, *quid mihi Celsus agit?* 'How is C. getting on, I should like to know?' For the scansion of *cuius*, here a monosyllable, see 'Metre', p. xxx.

150. Note the emphatic sound of the five spondees in this line. **nilo.** The word for 'nothing' in Latin is a compound of *ne*, 'not', and *hilum*, 'a jot'. It has four forms: the declinable *nihilum* and its contraction *nilum* (used only by Lucr.), the indeclinable *nihil* and its contraction *nil*. **divinitus,** 'by divine agency'.

151. quippe, 'for'. The emphasis of this sentence is on the *quod* clause: tr. 'For the reason why fear so grips all mortals is that . . .'.

152. multa . . . quorum operum: tr. as *multa opera* ('phenomena') . . . *quorum*; cf. *ea quae . . . corpora* II. 134 n. (extract no. 10). **tuentur,** 'behold', 'observe'; *tueor* is used by Lucr. and Vergil quite often in this, its primary meaning, by other writers only in its secondary meaning 'protect'.

153. ratione: see n. on *rationem* I. 51 (extract no. 2).

154. ac fieri . . . rentur (from *reor*), 'and think that they are brought about. . . .'; the acc. subject of *fieri* must be understood from *quorum* in the previous line. Lucr. not infrequently continues a relative clause with a co-ordinate clause in which the relative pronoun no longer has a construction in the case in which it stands.

156. sequimur, 'seek'.

157. **quaeque**: fem. sing. with *res*.

158. **quaeque**: neut. plur. = *omnia*. **operā**: governed by *sine*.

159. **omnibu'**: see 'Style', p. xxiv.

160. **semine** here has not the technical sense of 'atom', but the quite general meaning 'seed'.

161. **mare**: abl. Elsewhere Lucr. always uses the normal *mari*, but *mare* as an abl. occurs in Plautus and Ovid. What was said about *fragmina* ('Language', p. xxvi) applies here also. **homines**: sc. *possent oriri*.

162. **volucres**: sc. *possent*. **erumpere caelo**, 'burst forth from the sky', instead of breeding in a nest. Alternatively the sentence may be punctuated with a comma after *volucres* and no punctuation after *caelo* and *ferarum*: *posset* then has for its subject *genus et volucres* (cf. *videtur* V. 1189 n., extract no. 29), and the collective sing. *genus omne* (163) is the subject of the plur. *tenerent*—a common enough *constructio ad sensum*. This gives the sense 'men from the sea, fish and birds from the land, beasts from the sky'.

164. **incerto partu**, 'with uncertain birth', i.e. 'with no fixed law of birth' (Bailey). **culta ac deserta**: sc. *loca*.

165. **idem**: nom. plur. **arboribus**: dat. with *constare* = 'be consistent with'.

166. **omnes**: sc. *arbores*.

6. The Invisibility of Atoms (I. 265–89)

265. **nunc age**: Lucr. regularly uses this formula of transition to a new topic. **docui**, 'I have shown'.

267. **qua forte**, 'by any chance'; a rare instance of *forte* not as an adv., but as a noun with adj. in agreement. **coeptes**: present subjunctive of *coepto*, a frequentative formation, but meaning no more than 'begin'. **dictis**, 'my words'.

269. **accipe**, 'learn'. **tute necessest confiteare**, 'you yourself must admit': see n. on I. 146 (extract no. 5); *tute* is a more emphatic form of *tu*.

271. See 'Style', pp. xxiv and xxv.

272. **ruit** is transitive here and in 289, 'overwhelms'.

273. **campos** is the object of both *percurrens* and *sternit*, 'scouring the plains . . . strews them . . .'.

274. **supremos**: poetic for *summos*, 'tops of'.

275. **silvifragis**, 'forest-rending': one of Lucretius' most effective coinages; it occurs nowhere else.

277. **venti**: gen. sing., lit. 'there are of the wind invisible particles', tr. 'the wind consists of . . .'.

278. Anaphora (repetition of a word at the beginning of successive clauses) is a common rhetorical alternative to coordination in Latin.

279. **subito**: adj. with *turbine*. **vexantia . . . raptant**: both verbs govern the same objects as *verrunt*, 'tear and harry them'.

280. **nec ratione . . . alia . . . et cum**, 'and . . . in the same way as when' (lit. 'and not in another way than when'); *et* is found in prose with the meaning 'as' or 'than', though less commonly than *atque* or *ac*.

281. **mollis** is nom. agreeing with *natura*: see 'Style', p. xxv.

282. **flumine abundanti**: abl. of manner, 'in overflowing stream'.

284. **fragmina**: see 'Language', p. xxvi. **coniciens** agrees with *mollis aquae natura* (281). See also 'Metre', p. xxix. **arbusta,** 'trees': although *arbustum* really means 'plantation', its plural is often used in hexameter verse as a synonym for the metrically impossible *ārbŏrēs*.

286. **imbri**: abl.

287. **molibus**: dat. with *incurrit,* the 'piles' or 'piers' of a bridge.

288. **dat**, 'causes'; Lucr. often uses *do* in the sense of 'perform' an action denoted by a verbal noun.

289. **ruitque et quidquid**: Bailey's conjecture for the MS. reading *ruitque qua quidquid;* -*que* joins *volvit* and *ruit*, *et* joins *grandia saxa* and *quidquid fluctibus obstat*. Bailey tr. 'and rolls and dashes beneath its waves huge rocks and all that bars its flood'.

7. The Poem's Purpose (I. 921–50)

921. quod superest: not adverbial as in I. 50 (extract no. 2), but the object of *cognosce*. **clarius** is an adv., but the meaning is 'listen on a loftier plane' rather than 'hear more clearly'; Bailey tr. 'hear a loftier theme'.

922. me animi fallit, 'I am unaware' (lit. 'it escapes me in mind'): *animi* locative; the subject of *fallit* is the reported question *quam sint obscura*. **sint obscura**: as if *quod superest* in the previous line had been *quae supersunt*.

923. Note the emphatic sound of the four spondees, followed by *măgna mèúm còr*: see 'Metre', p. xxxii. **percussit,** 'inspired'; normally *percutio* means 'strike' physically. **thyrso,** 'goad' or 'spur'. The word really means the wand carried by Bacchus and his votaries; hence it comes to be associated with magic feats and 'inspired' energy. The sentiment is echoed by Milton, *Lycidas*, ll. 70–72:

> Fame is the spur that the clear spirit doth raise
> (That last infirmity of Noble mind)
> To scorn delights, and live laborious dayes.

924. incussit: see n. on *incutiens* I. 19 (extract no. 1); unlike *percutio, incutio* is normally figurative. **mi** = *mihi*: see n. on *omnibus* I. 19 (extract no. 1).

925. mente vigenti: with *instinctus* rather than *peragro*, 'by which inspired with strength of mind'.

926. avia: not 'pathless' (which is *invius*), but 'out of the way', 'off the beaten track', 'remote': i.e. philosophy is a rare subject for poetry. Certainly no Roman poet had taken philosophy as his theme, though the Greek philosophers Parmenides and Empedocles had both written in verse. **Pieridum** (*Pĭ-ĕ-rĭ-*), 'of the Muses', who were born in Pieria at the foot of Mt. Olympus: cf. Pope's well-known lines (*Essay on Criticism*, ll. 215–16):

> A little learning is a dang'rous thing:
> Drink deep, or taste not the Pierian spring.

927. sŏlo, 'foot': both 'sole' and 'soil' are meanings and derivatives of *solum*. **iuvat**: sc. *me*. Lucretius' proud boast that he was a pioneer in the fields of didactic poetry was copied—somewhat illogically—by Vergil in *Georgics* III. 291–3:

> *sed me Parnasi deserta per ardua dulcis*
> *raptat amor: iuvat ire iugis, qua nulla priorum*
> *Castaliam molli devertitur orbita clivo.*

integros, 'untasted'; N.B. *in-teg-ros*: see 'Metre', p. xxx.

929. **inde . . . unde**, 'from places whence'.

930. **nulli** = *nemini*, the usual dat. with parts of the body (*tempora* = 'temples' of the head): cf. *mi* (924). **velarint**: subjunctive of result, because *inde* is generic in meaning ('from places such that from them . . .').

931. **artīs**: abl. plur. of *artus -a -um*.

932. **religionum**: see n. on *religione* I. 63 (extract no. 3). This passage is cited by Lactantius in support of the view that *religio* is derived from *religo*, 'bind back', not (as Cicero thought) from *relego*, 'read over again'. Lucr. clearly regarded religion as that which shackles the mind.

933. **deinde**: see 'Metre', p. xxx.

934. **contingens**: here, and in 938 and 947, used in a quite literal sense, 'touching'.

935. **ab nulla ratione**, 'without (lit. proceeding-from no) reason'; see n. on *rationem* I. 51 (extract no. 2).

936. **pueris.** This is the normal Latin word for 'children' in the sense of 'boys and girls'; *liberi* means 'sons and daughters'. **absinthia taetra**, 'nasty wormwood'. **medentes** = *medici*.

937. **oras**, 'rims': cf. n. on *luminis oras* I. 22 (extract no. 1). **pocula circum**, 'round the cups'.

939. **puerorum aetas improvida** ('unsuspecting'): see 'Style', p. xxv. **ludificetur**: note the pentasyllabic ending: see 'Metre', p. xxxiii.

940. **labrorum tenus**, 'as far as the lips'; *tenus* always follows the word it governs, which is more often abl. than gen. N.B. *lab-ro-rum*.

941. **deceptaque non capiatur**, 'and, though tricked, be not harmed'. The use of *non* in a purpose clause is quite regular if it negatives a single word only. For this meaning of *capio* cf. Livy XXII. 2. 11, *ipse Hannibal altero oculo capitur* ('loses the sight of one eye').

942. **tali pacto**, 'by such means'; see n. on *quo pacto* I. 84 (extract no. 4).

943. **ratio**, 'doctrine' or 'system of philosophy', as in I. 51 (extract no. 2) etc.

944. **tristior**, 'rather unpalatable'. **quibus**, 'to those by whom'; *quibus* is dat. of agent, used only with the gerundive in prose, but with other parts of the passive in verse; its antecedent is an understood *iis*, dat. dependent on *videtur*: the omission of a part of *is* which would have been in the same case as the relative pronoun is in accordance with normal usage.

945. **suaviloquenti**: see 'Language', p. xxvi and 'Metre', p. xxxiii.

947. **quasi**, 'as it were'.

948. **si ... possem**, 'in the hope that I might be able ...'. A clause introduced by *si* ('in the hope that', 'to see if', 'in case') with its verb in the subjunctive is often found dependent on an idea of trying or waiting: it is generally classed as a reported question. Note that the imperfect subjunctive is used, even though *volui* (945) is best rendered 'I have wished': see n. on *esset* IV. 26 (extract no. 20). **ratione** here = *pacto* (942); so in I. 77 (extract no. 3) etc.

949. **omnem** etc., 'in what pattern the whole universe stands framed'. There are two objects of *perspicis*: (i) *omnem naturam rerum*, (ii) the reported question *qua ... figura*, of which the understood subject is (i) in the nom. This is a Greek idiom, of which an example translated literally into Eng. is 'I know thee who thou art' (Mark i. 24, A.V. and R.V.) It is more natural in Eng. to express (i) only as the subject of (ii).

950. **constet**: the word denotes lasting existence, 'stand firm', 'abide'. **compta**: *como* (*co-emo*) means (i) 'bring together', 'construct', 'compose', the basic meaning, but found only in Lucr.; (ii) 'arrange' (the hair), 'braid', 'comb', the predominant signification of the word; (iii) 'adorn' in general, but always as a conscious extension of (ii). The noun *comptus* occurs twice in Lucr., in senses

corresponding to meanings (i) and (ii) of the verb: (i) 'union' III. 845 (extract no. 17), (ii) 'tresses' I. 87 (extract no. 4).

8. The Blessedness of Epicurean Philosophy (II. 1–33)

1. **suave:** sc. *est.* **mari magno:** either (i) local abl., 'on the open sea', *turbantibus . . . ventis* being temporal, or (ii) abl. of attendant circumstances, 'when the sea is high', *turbantis . . . ventis* then being causal. **aequora,** 'its surface': see n. on I. 8 (extract no. 1).

2. **laborem,** 'struggles'.

3. **non quia:** here with indicative; normally a clause of rejected reason has subjunctive, e.g. II. 336 (extract no. 12). **vexari quem-quam,** 'for anyone to (that anyone should) be distressed': noun phrase subject of *est*.

4. Begin *sed quia . . . .* **quibus ipse malis careas** = *ea mala quibus ipse careas* ('one is free', subjunctive of indefinite 2nd person).

6. **tua sine parte pericli,** 'without sharing the danger oneself': *tua* (referring to the indefinite subject of *careas*) is used in the sense of a subjective gen., unlike *suo* I. 91 n. (extract no. 4); for *pericli* see 'Metre', p. xxx.

7. After *nil dulcius est* take *quam . . . tenere . . . templa; templa* has three attributes—(i) *bene munita,* (ii) *edita doctrinā sapientum,* (iii) *serena*.

8. **sapientum:** *metri gratia* for the normal *sapientium,* cf. n. on *animantum* I. 4 (extract no. 1). **templa,** 'dwellings'. The word *templum,* derived from a root *tem-* found in the Greek verb 'cut' (whence *tmesis* and *a-tomos,* 'indivisible'), was a technical term in augury, meaning either (i) the portion of ground marked off for the taking of the auspices, or (ii) the portion of the sky marked off for observation. From (i) developed the familiar sense of 'shrine', 'temple'; from (ii) the sense very common in Lucr., especially in the plur., of 'quarters' of the sky, e.g. VI. 388 (extract no. 31), 'regions' in general, e.g. III. 25 (extract no. 15), 'abodes' of divine beings, e.g. V. 948 (extract no. 26), and V. 1188 (extract no. 29), 'abodes' in general, e.g. the present passage. Another meaning ('cross-beam', 'rafter') occurs in line 28 of this extract: it has been suggested that this is the primary meaning of the word (i.e. a cut piece of wood), and that it came to be used first of the augur's 'hut', made of such beams, then of the 'augural field' on earth or in the

sky. If this theory is true, the sense here of 'dwelling' may arise directly from the architectural use of the word, rather than as an extension of its religious use.

9. **queas** : subjunctive both for the same reason as *careas* (4) and because it expresses purpose, *unde* being equivalent to *ut inde*. The infinitives in lines 9–13 fall into three groups : (i) *despicere* and *videre* depend on *queas*; (ii) *errare, quaerere, certare, contendere* and *niti* depend on *videre*; (iii) *emergere* and *potiri* depend on *niti*. **passim** : with *errare*.

11. **nobilitate,** 'claims of birth' (Bailey).

12. **praestante** : abl. in *-ĕ metri gratia*; *-ī* is normal when the participle is used purely as an adj., e.g. *abundanti* I. 282 (extract no. 6), *vigenti* I. 925 (extract no. 7).

13. **rerum,** '(political) power'; in this phrase *potior* always takes gen., otherwise gen. or abl., but the latter more commonly.

14. **mentis . . . pectora** : acc. of exclamation.

16. **hoc aevi quodcumquest,** 'this little span of years' (Bailey): cf. Catullus I. 8 *quicquid hoc libelli*. **nonne videre** (*sc. homines*), '(to think) that men should not see . . .!' This inf. of exclamation (with or without a subject) is found in prose and verse: e.g. Cic. *Pro Clu.* 15, *nonne timuisse . . . illam ipsam noctem . . .?* Verg. *Aen.* I. 37, *mene incepto desistere victam?*

17. **sibi . . . latrare,** 'demands for itself'; Lucr. follows Ennius in using *latro*, 'bark', in this sense. **utqui,** 'that somehow'; *qui* as an interrogative adv. ('how', 'why') is quite common: here *-qui* is the same adv. in an indefinite sense, cf. *atqui*, 'but somehow'.

18. **corpore** : abl. of separation with both *seiunctus* and *absit*. **mente fruatur** etc., 'and that, withdrawn from care and fear, she may enjoy in mind the sense of pleasure' (Bailey). N.B. (i) the asyndeton of *absit*, . . . *fruatur* is quite natural in view of the anti-thesis between *corpore* and *mente*, even though they are different uses of the abl.; (ii) *mente* is abl. of respect; (iii) the subject of *fruatur* is *natura* understood, and with this *semota* agrees; (iv) the abl. governed by *fruatur* is *iucundo sensu*; (v) *cura* and *metu* are abl. of separation; (vi) with *cura semota metuque* cf. *semotum a curis* I. 51 n. (extract no. 2).

20. **pauca ... esse opus,** 'that few things are necessary'. A nom. instead of the more strictly grammatical abl. with *opus est* is not uncommon in prose (e.g. Cic. *De Inv.* II. 57, *eius nobis exempla permulta opus sint*), and is in fact the normal usage if what is needed is expressed as a neut. adj. or pronoun. Here, of course, the nom. has become acc. in a reported statement.

21. **quae demant cumque,** 'just such as may remove'. N.B. (i) the clause is in apposition to *pauca*, (ii) the tmesis of *quaecumque* (see 'Style', p. xxv), (iii) the subjunctive expresses result ('things of such a kind that they remove . . .').

22. The punctuation, and consequent interpretation, of lines 21–23 are much disputed, but the general sense of the passage is clear enough: but few things are sufficient not only to remove pain from the body, but also to supply such simple positive pleasures as it needs. With the text given line 22 must be taken as another result clause, parallel to *quae demant cumque dolorem*, but introduced by *uti* instead of the relative pronoun. In tr. omit *uti* and co-ordinate the two clauses, 'and can also spread for our use many delights'.

23. **gratius** (sc. *quicquam*), 'nor does human nature itself from time to time need anything more acceptable' (Bailey). This line is the main clause of a long sentence extending to the end of the extract, the gist of which is: 'Even if wealth and luxury are lacking (24–28), yet (*tamen*) when men enjoy the beauties of Nature (29–31), especially in spring and summer (32–33), human nature needs no more (23).' Note that Calverley in his translation follows a different interpretation, taking 23 with what precedes. **ipsa :** i.e. when not 'spoilt' by luxuries.

25. **lampadās :** Greek form of 3rd decl. acc. plur. These lines are modelled on part of Homer's description of the palace of Alcinous, *Odyssey* VII. 100–2: 'Youths of gold, fixed on stout pedestals, held flaming torches in their hands to light the banqueters in the hall by night' (tr. E. V. Rieu).

27. **fulgēt.** The metrical licence of lengthening in the first syllable of a foot a vowel normally short is quite common in Vergil, but Lucr. has only two instances, the other being *scirēt* V. 1049 (extract no. 28). Both involve the 3rd pers. sing. active ending, of which the vowel was long in old Latin.

28. **citharae**: dat. with *reboant*, 'resound to the lyre'. **templa**, 'rafters': see n. on 8 above.

29. **inter se**, 'with one another', 'in groups'.

30. **propter**: cf. I. 90 n. (extract no. 4).

31. **opibus**, 'cost'. **corpora curant**, 'refresh themselves': *corpus curo* is a common phrase implying to take food and rest.

33. **tempora**, 'season'.

9. The Dance of the Atoms (II. 80–99)

80. **cessare**, 'stay still'. **rerum primordia**: see n. on I. 55 (extract no. 2).

82. **avius**, 'astray': cf. *avia* I. 926 n. (extract no. 7). **ratione**, 'reasoning'.

83. **vagantur** refers to the random movement of atoms—quite a different sense from that in which the word is used in the previous line, where it means to stray from the truth. **necessest**, 'it must be that . . .', with acc. and inf. instead of subjunctive as in I. 146 (extract no 5) and I. 269 (extract no. 6).

84. **ferri**: middle voice, 'move'.

85. **forte**, 'at times', whereas *gravitas* is a constant force. **alterius**: subjective gen., 'from another'. **cum . . . saepe**, 'whenever': the full meaning is *cum, ut saepe fit*, ... **cita**: a true perfect participle (of *cieo*), 'being in motion',' as they move'.

86. **obvia**, 'with one another'. **diversa**, 'in different directions'.

87. **neque . . . mirum**: sc. *est*. **durissima quae sint**, 'since they are perfectly hard': relative clause of reason.

88. **ponderibus**, 'mass'. **neque quicquam . . . obstet.** The relative clause is continued, though *quae* no longer has any construction in it: cf. n. on I. 154 (extract no. 5). **ibus**: see 'Language', p. xxvii. Atoms can leap apart in all directions after collision for two reasons: (i) they are completely solid, unlike compound bodies, the hardest of which has some admixture of *inane*; (ii) they are moving in a void, and there is therefore no obstacle to their movement till they meet another atom.

89. **quo . . . magis . . . pervideas,** 'that you may more clearly see'.

90. **corpora** see n. on I. 55 (extract no. 2). **reminiscere:** Lucretius' proof that the universe is infinite occurred earlier (I. 951–1007). **totius . . . in summa,** 'in the whole of the universe'; *totius* gen. of *totum* used as a noun = *omne* I. 74 (extract no. 3); *summa* is also a noun, 'the sum', 'the whole'. **imum nil,** 'no bottom'.

91. **neque habere** etc., 'and that the atoms have nowhere to rest'. From *corpora prima* (nom. in the *ubi* clause) the same words must be understood in the acc. as the subject of *·habere*: cf. I. 16 (extract no. 1), where the subject of the main clause must be understood from the object of the dependent clause.

93. **immensumque patere . . . ostendi,** 'and I have shown . . . that it spreads out immeasurable': *immensum* agrees with an acc· *spatium* understood from the nom. *spatium* in the previous line.

94. **pluribus:** sc. *verbis.* **ratione:** as in 82.

95. **quod . . . constat,** 'that is certain'. **nulla quies est:** see 'Metre', p. xxxii.

96. **reddita,** 'granted'.

97. **sed magis,** 'but rather'; *magis* modifies not *assiduo*, but all the rest of the sentence. **exercita,** 'driven on'.

98. **partim . . . pars,** 'some . . . others'. **intervallis magnis:** with *resultant.* **confulta:** middle voice, 'having clashed together'. The word does not occur elsewhere in Latin.

99. **vexantur,** 'are driven': *vexo* is in origin the frequentative of *veho.* **ab,** 'from' or perhaps 'as a result of', as in I. 935 n. (extract no. 7). When atoms collide, they either leap far apart or rebound only a short distance. Lucr. then proceeds to show (lines 100 sqq.) that the latter form hard bodies, the former soft ones, while those which do not combine move through space as 'free' atoms.

10. An Illustration of Atomic Movement (II. 112–41)

112. **cuius . . . rei:** i.e. that there are still many 'free' atoms which have not formed compounds, as Lucr. has stated just before this

extract. For *cuius*, which here has its normal pronunciation, see Metre', p. xxix; *rei* (normally scanned *rĕ-ī*) is in Lucr. always either *rē-ī* (as here) or a monosyllable by synizesis. **uti memoro,** 'as I say' present used colloquially (as in Eng.) for 'as I have said'. No doubt, as Lucr. wrote the preceding section on the behaviour of atoms, the vision of the motes with which he intended to illustrate it was so vivid in his mind that he forgot he had not already mentioned it. **simulacrum et imago** are no more than synonyms, precisely as 'image and likeness' are in Genesis i. 16.

113. **nobis:** see n. on *omnibus* I. 19 (extract no. 1). **instat,** 'is present'.

114. **contemplator:** 2nd pers. sing. of the Second (often called Future) Imperative of *contemplor*. This form of the imperative was commonly used in legal contexts, and so carries a touch of solemnity. Vergil imitates the usage in *Georgics* I. 187 and IV. 61. **cum . . . cumque:** tmesis, 'whenever': the word does not occur elsewhere. **solis lumina:** object of *fundunt*.

115. **inserti,** 'let in'. **opaca domorum** = *opacas domos*, a favourite periphrasis of Lucr., cf. I. 86 n. (extract no. 4).

116. **inane** here means 'the empty air', not 'the void', and *corpora* in the next line 'specks of dust' not 'atoms'; but the use of both words is a subtle reminder of the analogy which is being drawn throughout.

118. **proelia pugnas:** asyndeton, cf. *ferae pecudes* I. 14 n. (extract no. 1).

119. **dare pausam,** 'cease': see n. on dat I. 288 (extract no. 6.)

120. **conciliis et discidiis,** 'meetings and partings': two apt technical terms created by Lucr. to express the union and dissolution of atoms in a compound body.

121. **conicere,** 'guess' here: for the scansion see 'Metre', p. xxix. **primordia rerum . . . iactari:** noun phrase subject of *sit*, cf. *vexari quemquam* II. 3 n. (extract no. 8); tr. 'what it is for the atoms to be tossed'.

122. **inani,** 'the void' once more.

123. **dumtaxat,** 'at least', 'in some degree'. The contrast in

meaning between *rerum magnarum* and *parva res*, emphasized by
the juxtaposition of the adjectives, is echoed by the contrast in
sound between the spondees of the first four feet and the rapid and
irregular rhythm of *părva pòtést rès*: cf. I. 923 n. (extract no. 7).

124. **exemplare**: an archaic form, not found elsewhere, of
exemplar. **notitiai**, 'a general concept'. Just as Newton's imagination
leapt from the observation of a single apple falling in his mother's
garden to the idea of the same force acting upon the moon and so
to the concept of a universal gravitational force, so Leucippus, or
some other atomist, proceeded from the sight of moving motes in
particular sunbeam to the general theory of atoms endlessly moving
in space.

125. **hoc**, 'for this reason': lit. 'by this much', abl. of measure of
difference with *magis*, referring forward to the *quod*-clause beginning
in l. 127. **magis . . . par**, 'more right'. **haec animum te advertere . . . corpora**, 'for you to give heed to these bodies', noun
phrase subject of *est*: *advertere* governs the acc. *animum*, and the
combined phrase (often shortened to *animadvertere*) governs a
second acc. (here *haec*).

126. **turbare**, 'to make a disturbance': this absolute use of *turbo*
is found in other authors besides Lucr. **videntur**, 'are seen',
whereas the atoms are invisible (*caecus* 128 and 129).

129. **ibi**, i.e. *in solis radiis*.

130. **retro**, here *ret-ro*: the normal *rĕ-tro* is found in VI. 381
(extract no. 31).

132. **hic**, see 'Metre', p. xxix. **principiis**, see 'Language',
p. xxviii. **omnibus**, dat. with *est*: 'they all (i.e. the motes) have
this motion . . .'.

134. **ea quae . . . corpora**: tr. as *ea corpora quae*. . . . The trans-
ference to the relative clause of the noun which would in Eng. be
the antecedent is a very common Latin idiom, here seen in its
simplest form. **parvo sunt . . . conciliatu**, 'are formed by a small
union': *conciliatus* (see 'Language', p. xxvi) is the act of forming a
concilium (120 n.).

135. **quasi**, 'as it were'. **vīrīs**, acc. plur. of *vis*.

137. **proporro,** 'in their turn'.

138. **exit,** 'issues'. The actual movement of atoms is invisible, as is the source of that movement—the collision of the atoms. But a double process is at work to enable objects to be seen, as in the case of the motes in a sunbeam. Firstly, the atoms gather together to form larger bodies which eventually become visible. Secondly, as they do so, the motion of the atoms themselves is slowed down so as to render the objects which they form capable of perception.

139. **ut :** result, 'so that'.

141. **nec . . . apparet aperte,** 'though it is not clearly apparent'. see notes on I. 154 (extract no. 5) and II. 88 *neque quicquam obstet* (extract no. 9).

11. The Swerve of the Atoms (II. 216–24)

216. **illud** refers forward to the acc. and inf. *corpora* (217) . . . *depellere* (219); cf. I. 80 n. (extract no. 4). **avemus,** 'I wish'.

217. **corpora** here again = 'atoms'. **deorsum :** see 'Metre', p. xxx. **rectum per inane,** 'straight through the void': by a kind of hypallage, the notion 'straight' is expressed not adverbially, but as an adj. agreeing with *inane*. **feruntur :** cf. *ferri* II. 84 n. (extract no. 9).

218. **ferme,** 'quite' with *incerto* and *incertis*.

219. **spatio,** 'from their course'. **depellere** is here intransitive, 'swerve': Lucr. quite often uses in a middle or intransitive sense sense active forms of a verb normally transitive.

220. **tantum quod,** 'just so much as'. **momen mutatum,** 'change of direction': *momen* = *momentum*. **dicere,** 'call'. **possis :** subjunctive (i) in a relative clause of result (*quod* = *ut id*), (ii) of indefinite 2nd person.

221. **declinare,** 'swerve', the usual term for this in Lucr. and Cicero; unlike *depello* (219), *declino* is frequently used intransitively in the active by writers other than Lucr. **deorsum** is disyllabic again.

223. **foret** (= *esset*) . . . **natus** (almost = *factus*). Note the change of tense from *caderent*: the atoms would still be falling and no

collision would have taken place. **offensus** : see 'Language', p. xxvi.

224. principiis : a 'Lucretian' dative, going grammatically with *natus* and *creata*, but in sense equivalent to a gen. with *offensus* and *plaga*: cf. *rebus* I. 58 n. (extract no. 2).

12. The Variety of Atomic Shapes (II. 333–70)

333. deinceps : see 'Metre', p. xxx. **exordia** = *primordia*: either nom. subject of *sint* or acc. in the main clause as *omnem naturam* I. 949 n. (extract no. 7).

335. multigenis, 'manifold': only found here, but Lucr. uses other compound adj. in -*gena*.

336. non quo, 'not because', introducing a clause of rejected reason with normal subjunctive, unlike *non quia* II. 3 n. (extract no. 8). **multa parum,** 'only a few': the caesura helps to show that *parum* does not go with *simili*.

337. vulgo, 'without exception'. **paria omnibus omnia,** 'all like one another'. For the repetition of a word in a different case, where Eng. would use a different word, cf. Cic. *De Rep.* VI. 24, *mens cuiusque is est quisque,* 'each man's mind is the man himself'. **constant** = *sunt*: cf. *constet* I. 950 n. (extract no. 7).

338. nec mirum : sc. *est*.

340. omnibus : dat. depending on *pari* and *simili* in the next line; tr. 'one another' again. **omnia prorsum,** 'absolutely all': see 'Language', p. xxvii.

341. filo, 'build' (lit. 'texture'). **adfecta** = *praedita*.

342. Lines 342–6 consist of a series of subjects with no predicate, as if Lucr. intended to write *inter se differunt figuris*, but broke off after *pervolitantes*, picking up the nominatives with *quorum* (347). A rigorously grammatical sentence would begin with a list of genitives instead of the nominatives, but this would be hopelessly clumsy. As it is, the anacoluthon is elegant and can be left in translation.

343. squamigerum : here a noun in the gen. plur. In I. 162 (extract no. 5) the same form was a nom. sing. neuter adj. **pecudes,**

'shoals': normally *pecus pecoris* is the collective noun and *pecus pecudis* denotes the individual creature.

344. **laetantia**: tr. by Bailey 'gladdening', as from the rare active verb *laeto*, but may be from the much commoner deponent *laetor*, 'rejoice', the emotion of the beholder being transferred by hypallage to the scene that provokes it: so *laeta* is applied to *pabula* I. 14 (extract no. 1) and II. 364 below, and to *arbusta* II. 594 (extract no. 13). **quae lŏca aquărum**: this irregularity in the rhythm of the last two feet—three instead of two word-stresses, but clash with ictus avoided by the use of a monosyllable to begin the 5th foot— recurs twice in this passage, 357 and 371.

345. **concelebrant**: cf. I. 4 n. (extract no. 1).

346. **pervulgant**, 'haunt'. **avia**: cf. I. 926 n. (extract no. 7).

347. **quorum**, 'of these', neuter referring collectively to all the preceding nominatives: so also *unum quidvis*. **generatim**, 'kind by kind'. **sumere perge**, 'go on taking': i.e. having finished one kind, go on to the next.

348. **differre**: the subject is understood, 'that individuals differ'. Lucr. does not really make explicit his point, which is, of course, the difference not between kinds (*genus humanum*, *squamigeri*, *armenta*, etc.), nor between species within one kind, but between individual members of one species.

349. **ratione**, 'way', as in I. 77 (extract no. 3) etc.

350. **quod posse videmus**: sc. *eas* (*i.e. matrem et prolem*) *facere*, 'but we see that they can do this'.

351. **atque**, 'than'. **nota cluere**: sc. *omnia* (i.e. not merely *matrem et prolem*, but *unum quidvis*), 'that all these things are known apart'; *clueo*, a verb used mainly by Plautus and Lucr., normally means 'am called', 'am esteemed', but here 'show myself to be'—little more than 'am'.

353. **turicremas**, 'incense-burning', apparently coined by Lucr., but afterwards used by Vergil (*Aen.* IV. 453), Ovid (*Her.* II. 18), and Lucan (IX. 989). **propter**, 'beside', as in I. 90 (extract no. 4).

355. **peragrans**: here *pe-rag-rans*. The normal pronunciation is found in I. 74 (extract no. 3) and I. 926 (extract no. 7).

356. **quaerit** is Bailey's conjecture for the MS. *non quit*. Other suggestions are *noscit* and *novit*. **pedibus . . . bisulcis,** 'cloven hoofs'. **pressa,** 'marked'.

357. **si**: see n. on I. 948 (extract no. 7).

359. **adsistens,** 'standing still'. **crebră**: acc. plur. neuter used as adv. *metri gratia* instead of the normal *crebrō*. **revisit**: intransitive, 'returns'; more often the verb is transitive and means 'revisit', 'return to'; e.g. IV. 393 (extract no. 21).

360. **perfixa,** 'pierced'.

362. **illa,** 'well-known', 'familiar'. **summis ripis,** 'level with their banks'.

363. **subitam . . . curam,** 'the sudden pang of care': the cow's sense of loss, momentarily forgotten as she contemplates the grass and streams, suddenly recurs.

364. **vitulorum aliae species,** hypallage for *vitulorum aliorum species*: see 'Style', p. xxv. Other calves look different: this is the point of the passage.

365. **derivare,** 'divert': lit. to divert a stream (*rivus*) from its usual channel. **curaque levare,** 'and relieve it of care'.

366. **usque adeo,** 'so eagerly'. **proprium,** 'distinctive', i.e. peculiar to the calf. **notum,** 'familiar' to herself.

368. **norunt** = *noverunt*, 'know': perfect of *nosco* with present meaning, cf. *suemus* I. 60 n. (extract no. 2). **petulci,** 'butting'.

369. **balantum** (sc. *ovium*): cf. *animantum* I. 4 n. (extract no. 1). **quod** = *id quod*, 'as'. **natura,** 'their nature'.

370. **fere,** 'always': the sense of the passage demands more than the normal meaning 'generally'.

13. Nature's Variety Springs from Atomic Variety
(II. 581–99)

581. **illud**: cf. I. 80 n. (extract no 4) and II. 216 n. (extract no. 11). **obsignatum,** 'sealed', a metaphor from a legal document.

582. convenit, 'it is right'. **memori . . . mente :** for the metrically impossible *mĕmŏrĭā*. **mandatum,** 'stored'.

583. nil esse : sc. *eorum* (neuter), 'that there is none of those things, whose nature' etc. **in promptu,** 'before our eyes', 'manifestly'.

584. genere : here, as in 588, used as a technical expression for atoms which have the same shape.

585. semine : collective for *seminibus*; see n. on I. 55 (extract no. 2). **constet** = *consistat*.

586. magis . . . multas = *plures*. **vis :** acc. plur., 'forces'; the normal form *viris* occurs in II. 135 (extract no. 10) and V. 1017 (extract no. 27). **in se :** pronounced (like 'in it' in Eng.) as a single word accented on the first syllable. There is thus no clash of word-stress and ictus.

588. docet, 'shows': cf. *docui* I. 265 n. (extract no. 6).

589. principio, 'in the first place'. Lucretius' first example of a compound of many different kinds of atoms is the earth (589–99). This leads to a digression on the worship of Mother Earth or Cybele (600–45), followed by a statement of the Epicurean belief about the gods (646–60, extract no. 14). Only after this does Lucr. return to his main argument, and give further examples of diverse compounds.

590. frigora, 'coldness': i.e. *aquam frigidam*.

591. habet : anaphora, cf. I. 278 n. (extract no. 6). The object of *habet* is *corpora prima* understood from 589, and *ignes* is the subject of *oriantur*.

592. Note the clash of word-stress and ictus in this line: *năm mùltís succĕnsa lòcís àrdént sòla tĕrrae*. **sola,** 'the soil', 'the surface', as opposed to *ex imis* ('from the depths') in the next line.

593. impetus, 'eruption'. See extract no. 32 and commentary thereon, p. 102.

594. nitidas fruges arbustaque laeta gentibus humanis : all this is the object of *extollere* in the *unde* clause, but is placed early in the sentence for emphasis; *corpora prima* is again understood as the object of *habet* and antecedent of *unde*.

596. fluvios frondis et pabula : note the asyndeton between the nanimate *fluvios* and the two nouns denoting vegetation, them-selves coupled by *et*.

597. montivago, 'mountain-ranging', a favourite compound of Lucr.

598. magna . . . mater, 'the Great Mother', the title under which Cybele was worshipped at Rome.

599. nostri . . . corporis almost = *generis humani*. **haec . . . una**, 'she alone': note the emphatic position of *una*. **dicta est**: cf. *dicere* II. 220 n. (extract no 11).

14. The Truth about the Gods and Nature (II. 646–60)

649. privata, 'free'.

650. nil indiga nostri, 'having no need of us'.

651. nec bene promeritis capitur, 'is neither won over by good services'.

653. potĭtur: 3rd conj., as occasionally in other poets; always 4th conj. in prose. Note also that here the verb takes acc. instead of the normal gen. or abl., and means 'has possession of', not 'gains possession of'.

655. hic, 'herein'.

656. abuti, 'misuse': more often the word means 'use to the full', as in V. 1033 (extract no. 28).

657. laticis, 'grape juice'. **vocamen**: coined by Lucr. for *vocabulum*.

659. dum . . . tamen, 'provided however that'. **vera re . . . ipse**, 'truly in himself': *vera re* and *ipse* practically express the same mean-ing: he may follow convention, but his own true self must remain uncontaminated.

660. contingere parcat, 'forbear to contaminate', 'refrain from contaminating'.

15. In Praise of Epicurus (III. 1–30)

2. primus: see n. on *Graius homo* I. 66 (extract no. 3). The point is discussed further on p. 50. **inlustrans**, 'shedding light on'. **commoda**, 'joys', 'blessings'.

3. te sequor. Here, as always, Lucr. is an ardent disciple, with no other thought than to expound his master's teaching; the teaching maintained its rigid structure throughout the centuries, unlike the rival creed of Stoicism. **Graiae:** see 'Metre', p. xxix. **inque tuis . . . pressis . . . signis,** 'and in your well-marked tracks': cf. *pressa* II. 356 (extract no. 12). The 'excited' rhythm of the last two feet of 3—*ínque tùis nùnc*—recurs three times in this passage, lines 8, 17, and 29: see 'Metre', p. xxxii.

4. ficta (= *fixa*) **pedum** (sc. *meorum*) **. . . vestigia,** 'my firm footsteps': *fictus* was the original form of the perfect participle of *figo*; its meaning is stronger than *pressus*: cf. Cic. *Pro Sestio* 13, (*integritatis*) *vestigia non pressa leviter . . . sed fixa ad memoriam sempiternam.*

5. non ita . . . quam, 'not so much . . . as'. **propter amorem** balances *certandi cupidus* (though different in construction) and is amplified by *quod te imitari aveo.*

6. quid : adverbial, 'for how could . . .?' The questions are deliberative.

7. cycnis : the beauty of the supposed song of the dying swan was a commonplace of ancient poetry.

8. consimile . . . et fortis equi vis, 'to compare with the strong might of the horse', lit. 'like as the strong might of the horse (can do)'. For *et* meaning 'as', see n. on I. 280 (extract no. 6); *fortis* is better taken as nom. than gen., *fortis vis* balancing *tremulis artubus.*

9. pater . . ., rerum inventor : both complements of *es* in asyndeton, 'our father and the discoverer of truth'.

10. inclute, 'our hero' (Bailey). The adj. suggests that Epicurus is raised not merely to parental stature, but to an heroic and god-like level. 'He feels towards Epicurus as towards a saviour, and applies the language of religious intensity to the man whom he regards as the destroyer of religion' (Bertrand Russell, *A History of Western Philosophy*, p. 271). **chartis,** 'pages'.

11. libant, 'sip'. This is the primary meaning of the word—'to take a little of' as a taste. Commonly it means to pour a little of a liquid as an offering or 'libation' to the gods.

13. aurea : repeated for emphasis.

4. **ratio,** 'philosophy', as in I. 51 (extract no. 2) etc.

5. **coortă** agrees with *ratio*, 'sprung'.

6. **moenia mundi discedunt,** 'the walls of the world part', revealing the gods dwelling in the *intermundia*.

17. **geri res,** 'events happen': i.e. the ceaseless motion of the atoms.

18. **divum numen,** 'the majesty of the gods'.

20. **concreta,** 'congealed', lit. 'having grown together': perfect participle of *concresco* used in an active meaning.

21. **cana** goes closely with *cadens*, 'falling white'. **innubilus,** 'cloudless': the word occurs nowhere else in Latin (see p. 50).

22. **et . . . ridet:** see notes on *ac fieri . . . rentur* I. 154 (extract no. 5) and *neque quicquam . . . obstet* II. 88 (extract no. 9). Cf. also *rident* I. 8 n. (extract no. 1).

24. **animi pacem:** i.e. *ataraxia*. **delibat:** a compound of *libo* (see n. on 11 above), meaning 'take a little away from', and so 'detract from', 'diminish'.

25. **Acherusia templa,** 'the regions of Acheron': see n. on *templa* II. 8). Acheron, strictly one of the five rivers of the underworld, was often used to denote the underworld as a whole—or rather that part of it in which the guilty were punished.

26. **nec tellus obstat:** because the vision of Epicurus transcends physical barriers, cf. *moenia mundi discedunt* 16–17.

27. **geruntur:** as *geri* 17.

28. **his . . . rebus:** abl. of cause, 'at the thought of these things'. **ibi,** 'thereupon', 'then'. **voluptas . . . atque horror.** This kind of 'awe' has been referred to in the Introduction, p. xxi, as characteristic of the true scientist in the face of reality. It has been investigated on the religious side by R. Otto in his book *Das Heilige* (Eng. translation *The Idea of the Holy*), where the essence of religion is stated to lie in a combination of these two nearly opposite emotions which Lucr. here puts together. 'The demonic-divine object may appear to the mind an object of horror and dread, but at the same time it is no less something that allures with a potent charm, and the creature who trembles before it . . . has always at

the same time the impulse to turn to it, nay even to make it some-how his own' (op. cit., p. 31).

29. **percipit,** 'seizes'.

30. **manifesta patens:** N.B. (i) the adj. goes closely with the participle (cf. *cana cadens* 21 n.); (ii) the whole phrase is proleptic with *retecta est*, tr. 'has been uncovered and lies plain to view'.

16. The Mortality of the Soul (III. 417-44)

417. **nunc age:** cf. I. 265 n. (extract no. 6). **animantibus:** see notes on *animantum* I. 4 (extract no. 1) for the word and on *principiis* II. 224 (extract no. 11) for the case. **et mortalis:** note the spondee in the 5th foot.

419. **dulci . . . labore.** The putting together of two such dissimilar words is much more than a reminder that Lucr. enjoys hard work (and no doubt expects his readers to). They show that, for him, as for most classical poets, poetry was much more a 'skill' than an 'unpremeditated art'. Our expression 'work of art' perhaps faintly preserves the idea of art as hard work. And the Latin root of 'culture' takes us back to the farmer working his land. So, according to Lucr., must the poet labour to bring his medium of expression under cultivation.

420. **tua . . . vita:** merely a periphrasis for *te*, 'of yourself' (i.e. Memmius). **disponere**, 'set down', lit. 'arrange'.

421. **fac . . . iungas,** 'be sure to unite'. Soul and mind compose a single entity, and whichever term is used may be taken to include the other. This is an important but parenthetic argument, which would have been relegated to a footnote in a modern book.

422. **verbi causa,** 'to use a word': he must use one word or the other.

423. **dicere:** sc. *me*.

424. **quatenus**, 'since'. **unum inter se,** 'the same thing as the other': *inter se* is a very common way of expressing 'each other' in various relations, but is rare with a sing. subject. **coniuncta res,** 'a combined entity'.

425. principio. The first of Lucretius' twenty-nine proofs occupies the rest of this extract; the other twenty-eight occupy lines 445–829, which we do not include. The main verb of the sentence beginning at this line is *crede* (437), preceded by (i) the clause *quoniam* (425) . . . *fumus* (428), (ii) the parenthesis *nam* (428) . . . *geruntur* (433), (iii) the resumptive words *nunc igitur* (434) and the clause *quoniam* (434) . . . *auras* (436). **tenuem constare:** sc. *animam*, 'that the soul (is) fine (and) consists'; *tenuem* is predicative; *constare* has the same meaning as in II. 585 (extract no. 13). **minutis corporibus.** Lucr. has already shown (III. 177 sqq.) that the soul consists of minute particles. There the first argument for this minuteness was that 'the mind is moved more quickly than any of the things whose nature is manifest for all to see' (184–5). Here Lucr. again links minuteness with mobility, in order to show how easily the soul is dispersed when its containing vessel the body is destroyed.

427. liquidus umor aquai: the Lucretian periphrasis, see 'Style', p. xxv. The nom. after *quam* is strictly grammatical (sc. *est*), but unusual: if no verb is expressed, the noun after *quam* is usually attracted to the same case as the noun with which it is compared.

429. a, 'by': *a* and *ab* quite often mean 'proceeding from', 'as a result of', e.g. I. 935 (extract no. 7); with a passive verb the meaning is really no different from an instrumental abl. **tenui . . . magis,** 'slighter'.

430. quippe ubi . . . movetur, 'seeing that it is moved'. Lucr. several times uses the indicative in clauses preceded by *quippe,* but the subjunctive is more usual. **imaginibus:** soul and mind must consist of minute particles, firstly, because they can be stirred by the normal perception of something so vague and indefinite as to be almost imperceptible, e.g. cloud or smoke; secondly, and at an even greater remove from definiteness, because we may perceive an 'image' of smoke in sleep. This is a much more *tenuis causa* because the sense organs of sight are not then aroused. This has been a commonplace of psychology since Hume, who said: 'Images strike upon the mind with less liveliness than perceptions.'

431. quod genus: adverbial acc., 'as'. **alte,** 'on high', with *exhalare*.

432. ferre, 'send up'.

433. procul . . . dubio, 'without doubt'. **haec** is the subject and *simulacra* the complement of *geruntur*, which is here used as a copulative verb with an accessory idea of motion: tr. 'these are images borne to us'; *gero* meaning 'bear' or 'carry' with respect to the *terminus ad quem* is rare but not unparalleled (see Lewis & Short, s.v. I B 1): nevertheless Creech's emendation *feruntur* is attractive. **simulacra**: Lucr. uses this and *imagines* synonymously for Epicurus' *eidola* (εἴδωλα): cf. n. on *simulacrum et imago* II. 112 (extract no. 10). The Epicurean theory of images and vision is expounded in IV. 26–43 (extract no. 20). There are two sorts of image: visual images, which are thin films emanating from the surface of objects; and mental images, which are flimsier than visual ones, and by whose impact only mind-atoms are moved.

434. quoniam etc. This clause by presenting an analogy gives the reason why the reader may readily believe the truth of Lucretius' proposition (*animam . . . recessit*, 437–9); the *quoniam* clause preceding the parenthesis gives the reason for the proposition itself. **undique,** 'in all directions', with *diffluere*.

435. laticem discedere: a mere restatement of *diffluere umorem*.

439. ablata: *ab-la-ta*, see 'Metre', p. xxx.

440. quippe etenim corpus . . . cum, 'for indeed since the body . . .'; *cum* in a causal sense with the indicative, found also in Plautus and Terence, is paralleled by the Eng. use of 'when' with causal meaning (which would be a suitable tr. here). **quasi constitit,** 'was, so to speak'.

441. cohibere (sc. *animam*), 'hold it together'. **conquassatum,** 'if shattered'. **ex aliqua re,** 'from some cause'.

442. 'or rarefied by the withdrawal of blood from the veins'; *ac* is logical: the inability of the body to contain the soul is true of sudden death *and* of slow bleeding to death, but 'or' is more natural in Eng.

443. āĕrĕ: see n. on *aer* VI. 684 (extract no. 32). **qui credas,** 'how could you believe . . .?' **cohiberier** = *cohiberi*: see 'Language', p. xxvii.

444. This line contains a well-known crux. The MS. reading is *corpore qui nostro rarus magis incohibescit*. If that is what Lucr.

wrote, *qui* is the relative pronoun in the nom. sing. masc. (antecedent
ere) and *incohibesco* (otherwise unknown) must be an inceptive
compound of *cohibeo*, in which the prefix intensifies its meaning,
and the inceptive suffix adds a conative sense: 'which, (being) more
rare than our body, tries (*and by implication fails*) to hold (it, i.e. *the
soul*) in'. Most editors, however, consider that the line needs
emendation. In his 1947 edition Bailey 'with much hesitation'
adopted Woltjer's *incohibens sit*, which supposes an otherwise unknown *incohibeo*, in which the prefix is again intensive ('which is
more rare . . . as it holds it in'). But this is hardly satisfactory, since
the point of the passage is that air does *not* hold the soul in. Among
many other suggestions Lachmann's *is cohibessit* has found much
favour. Line 443 then ends with a question mark instead of a
comma, *qui* is an adv. in 444 as well as 443, and *cohibessit* is an
archaic present subjunctive of *cohibeo*, like *prohibessit* (Plautus,
Pseudolus 14), *ausim* (e.g. Lucr. V. 196 n., extract no. 24), etc.:
'How could that, (being) more rare . . ., hold (it) in?'

17. The Blessings of Mortality (III. 830–69)

830. **hilum**: *metri gratia* for *quicquam*; see n. on *nilo* I. 150
(extract no. 5).

831. **mortalis habetur**, 'is a mortal possession'.

832. **anteacto . . . tempore**, 'in time past'; see 'Metre', p. xxx. **nil
. . . aegri**, 'no pain'.

833. **ad confligendum**, 'to the conflict'.

834. **omnia**, 'all the world'.

835. **horrida**, 'shuddering'. **oris**: see n. on *luminis oras* I. 22 (extract no. 1).

836. **fuere**: the subject is still *omnia*. **utrorum**: *ut-ro-rum*.

837. **humanis**: probably masc. = *hominibus*, but possibly neuter,
'human power'.

839. **quibus e** = *e quibus*. **uniter apti**, 'joined in one'; *uniter* is a
coinage of Lucr., *apti* the perfect participle (and the only part in
actual use) of an obsolete verb *apo apere*.

841. **sensum . . . movere,** 'stir our senses'.

842. *ét màre caĕlo.*

843. At this point Lucr. leaves his main argument, returning to it in 862. **si iam,** 'supposing for a moment that'. The verb of the *si*-clause is *sentit*, of which the subject is *animi natura animaeque potestas*: a sing. verb having two sing. subjects joined by 'and' is not uncommon. The indicative is used, not because Lucr. believed this to be true, but because the main verb, *est* (845), is indicative. The explanation in 'Bradley's Arnold' § 452 Obs. 2[1] cannot be bettered: 'Nor does the mood of the *si*-clause depend upon the likelihood, unlikelihood, possibility or the reverse, of the supposition made; but simply on the mood . . . of the principal clause. Cicero says, *excitate eum, si potestis, ab inferis*; he did not think it possible that they could raise a man from the dead; yet he says *si potestis*, not *si possitis*.' **nostro . . . de corpore** belongs with *distractast* in the *postquam* clause.

845. **comptu,** 'union' (lit. 'putting together'): see n. on *compta* I. 950 (extract no. 7).

846. **uniter apti:** cf. 839 n.

847. **materiem nostram,** 'the matter of which we are made'. **collegerit,** '*should* gather together': a perfect subjunctive is sometimes found instead of the more usual pres. subjunctive in the protasis of a 'remote future' condition, if the action of that verb would be completed before that of the main verb. **aetas,** 'time'.

848. **ut sita nunc est,** 'into its present state'.

850. **id quoque factum** (sc. *esse*), 'that even this had been done'.

851. 'when once the recollection of ourselves had been broken off'. N.B. (i) the subjunctive *interrupta sit* is not due to *cum*, but is conditional—in the circumstances imagined, the chain of memory *would have been* broken; (ii) 'remote future' conditions are primary in Latin, but historic in English; (iii) *repetentia*, a Lucretian word.

852. **de nobis . . . ante qui fuimus,** 'about the selves that we once were'.

853. **illis:** i.e. our past selves.

[1] In the pre-1938 edition. In the 1938 revision the same point is made somewhat less forcibly in a note to § 451.

854. **respicias** (*a*) is subjunctive of indefinite 2nd person—cf.
careas II. 4 n. (extract no. 8)—not due to *cum*, (*b*) has two objects:
(i) *immensi temporis omne praeteritum spatium* (hypallage for *omne
immensum spatium temporis praeteriti*); (ii) the reported question
quam multimodis sint motūs materiai. In tr. it will be best to render
respicias separately with each object: 'For when one looks back over
the measureless expanse of past time, (and) then (considers) how
manifold are the motions of matter . . .'.

856. **multĭmodis** is an adv., but may here be rendered adjectivally.
It is *multī* modīs* with the first *i* shortened. **hoc** : see 'Metre', p. xxix.
possis, 'one can'.

857. **semina** is qualified by *haec eadem, quibus e nunc nos sumus* in
the next line. **posta** : see 'Metre', p. xxx.

859. **memori . ... mente** : cf. II. 582 n. (extract no. 13). **reprehendere**, 'recover', 'recall'.

860. **inter . . . iectast**, tmesis: 'has been interposed' or 'has
intervened'. **vitai pausa**, 'a break in life'. **vage**, 'far away': 'and
all the motions have everywhere wandered far away from the senses'
—i.e. after the dissolution of the body, mind, and soul, the motions
of the atoms which composed them continue, but no longer produce
the sensations which they did when combined.

861. **deerrarunt**, see 'Metre', p. xxx.

862. **enim** follows on from 842: Lucr. now returns to his main
argument. **misere si forte aegreque futurumst**, 'if by chance
there is to be grief and pain (for a man)' : for the adverbs with *sum*
cf. Catullus XXXVIII. 1–2:

> *male est, Cornifici, tuo Catullo,*
> *male est, me hercule, et laboriose.*

So also in the next line with *accidere*.

863. **ipse**, 'the man himself'. **esse** with *debet* in the previous line,
'must exist' : *debeo* here denotes not (as usually) moral duty, but
inevitability. **tum** strengthens *in eo tempore* : 'at that actual time'.
cui = *ut ei*, 'in order that ill may befall him'.

864. **eximit**, 'forestalls'. **esseque probet**, 'and prevents him
from existing' : see 'Metre', p. xxx.

865. 'the man to whom misfortunes could be attached': *possin.*
subjunctive of result, because the clause on which it depends (*esse*
probet illum) is virtually negative.

867. **nec . . .** (sc. *eum*) **qui non est posse,** 'and that he who does
not exist cannot . . .'. **neque hilum differre,** 'and that it makes not a
jot of difference': *differre* impersonal.

868. **an nullo** : before this *utrum aliquo* is understood, lit. '(whether)
he was born (at some time) or at no time up to now'; tr. 'whether
or not he has ever yet been born'.

869. **mors . . . immortalis,** 'death everlasting': a fine instance of
oxymoron, cf. Tennyson, *Idylls of the King*, *Lancelot and Elaine*,
ll. 871–2:

> His honour rooted in dishonour stood,
> And faith unfaithful kept him falsely true.

18. The Futility of Mourning (III. 894–911)

894. Take *aiunt* (898) early: ' "Very soon," men say, "your glad
home . . ." '.

896. **praeripere,** lit. 'be the first to snatch': the prolative infinitive
which is normal usage with verbs meaning 'hasten' is here extended
to *occurro*.

897. **factis florentibus** : abl. of attendant circumstances, 'in pros-
perity', 'prosperous'.

898. **aiunt** : see 'Metre', p. xxix.

900. **tibi . . . insĭdet** (pres. of *insideo*), 'abides with you'.

901. **desiderium** as always means 'longing' for what one has lost.
super, 'moreover'. **unā,** lit. 'together (with you in the grave)'; tr.
'still'.

902. **dictisque sequantur,** 'and followed it out in their words'.

903. **dissoluant,** 'they would free': see 'Metre', p. xxxi.

904–8. A second fallacy: though it is true that the dead man feels
no more, death is to be feared because of the sorrow it causes the
survivors.

904. **es leto sopitus,** 'have fallen asleep in death'. **aevi quod superest,** 'for all time to come': *aevi* partitive gen. dependent on an understood *id* (acc. of 'time how long'), lit. '(for that amount) of time which remains'.

905. **privatu',** 'released'. **doloribus aegris,** 'grievous pains'.

906. **horrifico . . . busto:** local abl., 'on the dreadful pyre'. Strictly *bustum* is the site on which the pyre (*rogus*) has been consumed. **prope:** adv., 'nearby'.

907. A most impressive hexameter built of three words, its solemnity enhanced by the 5th-foot spondee and quadrisyllabic ending. Even in quoting an argument which he is about to refute Lucr. does not spare his art.

909. **hoc,** 'such a man', 'one who speaks thus.' **quid sit amari tanto opere,** 'what is so very bitter (about this)': *amari* partitive gen. sing. neut. dependent on *quid*; *tanto opere* adv. of *tantus*.

910. **si res redit,** 'if it comes at last' to sleep and rest. The indicative shows that this clause depends on the main clause, not on the reported question.

911. **cur** introduces a relative clause of result: 'that therefore' anyone should . . . .

19. The Hereafter is Here (III. 978–1023)

978. **Acherunte:** local abl. See also n. on III. 25 (extract no. 15).

979. **prodita sunt esse,** 'are fabled to exist'.

980. **impendens** agrees with *saxum*. **aere:** local abl. going with *impendens*.

981. **Tantalus** had stolen the food and drink of the gods. According to Homer he was 'tantalized' by the presence of food and drink placed just out of his reach; but Lucr. refers to the version, more general among both Greek and Roman writers, that his torment was perpetual terror of a great rock poised over him: see, for instance, the quotation from Cicero in the note on V. 1186 (extract no. 29). **cassa,** 'idle' because the rock would never fall. **torpens,** 'numb'.

983. **casum:** a play on the two senses of the word, 'mischance' and the literal 'fall' of the rock. Bailey tr. 'the fall of the blow which

chance may deal to each'. Note the clash of word-stress and ictus in this line: *mórtàlis casŭmque tìmént quèm cuĭque fèrát fòrs.*

984. Tityon: the Greek form of the acc. is retained, as of the nom. in 992. For assaulting Latona the giant Tityos after death had his entrails eternally devoured by vultures. **ineunt,** 'probe'.

985. quod . . . scrutentur . . . quicquam, 'anything to grope for': relative clause of purpose. **sub,** 'deep in'.

986. perpetuam aetatem, 'for all eternity'.

987. 'However vast the mass of his outstretched limbs', (lit. 'with however vast an outstretch of body he may project'): *quamlìbet* as a substitute for *quamvis* with concessive subjunctive and the 4th decl. noun *proiectus* are both very rare.

988. qui . . . obtineat: concessive relative clause, 'though he cover . . .'. **dispessis:** perfect participle of *dispando*.

989. qui: omit in tr.

992-4. 'But we have T. here (on earth), "torn by vultures" as he grovels in love—that is to say (*atque*) devoured by aching anguish or rent by care through some other passion.'

992. in amore balances *Acherunte* (984).

993. exēst: from *exedo*.

994. cuppedine: see 'Language', p. xxvii.

995. *ánte òculós èst.*

996. petere . . . imbibit, 'pants in quest of'. **fascis . . . securis:** symbols of the highest civil and military power.

998. inane, 'an empty thing'. The 'Sisyphus' of our life is the man who, for all his efforts, never achieves power (*nec datur umquam*); but, adds Lucr. by the way, even those who do achieve it find it to be futile.

1000. hoc: see 'Metre', p. xxix. So also in 1008. **adverso . . . monte,** 'uphill'. **nixantem,** 'with great effort': the effort is suggested by the spondaic rhythm of the line.

1002. petit, 'makes for': the repeated *p, t,* and *c* sounds of the line suggest the thudding descent of the stone. **aequora**: see n. on I. 8 (extract no. 1).

1003. **pascere . . . atque explere,** 'to feed and to fill'.

1004. **satiareque numquam,** 'and (yet) never satisfy it': *and* may be adversative in Eng. e.g. Matt. xxi 30, '. . . said, I go, sir: and went not'.

1006. **fetus,** 'fruits'.

1008. **hoc . . . id est, . . . puellas quod memorant . . . congerere**: the object of *memorant* is *quod*, to which the acc. and inf. stands in apposition. In tr. supply another verb: 'this . . . is what (they mean when) they speak of maidens . . . pouring . . .'. The reference is to the daughters of Danaus, condemned for the murder of their husbands eternally to fill with water a vessel full of holes. **aevo florente,** 'in the flower of youth'.

1010. **potestur**: in early Latin *possum* and *queo* took passive forms with a passive inf., as *coepi* continued to do in classical Latin.

1011. Lines 1011–13, if accepted as they stand (as Bailey 'with some hesitation' does in his 1947 edition), present three difficulties: (i) the lack of a main verb (as in II. 342–6 n., extract no. 12, we have a series of nominatives followed by a relative clause, but here there is not the same justification for the anacoluthon); (ii) the asyndeton *egestas, Tartarus* (but cf. *ferae pecudes* I. 14 n., extract no. 1); (iii) the masc. gender of *qui* (though this is not too unnatural, since the first and last of the antecedents are masc.). Many editors prefer to suppose that between 1012 and 1013 one or more lines have been lost, containing the main verb (something like 'are described in legend') and at least one more subject, probably masc. (Cicero's *Cocyti fremitus, Tusc.* I. 10, would suit both sense and metre).

1012. **faucibus**: the 'jaws' of hell, i.e. such supposed entrances to the Underworld as that at Lake Avernus, by which Aeneas descended (Verg. *Aeneid* VI). **aestus,** 'vapours'.

1014. **in vita**: cf. 982 and 995.

1015. **est,** '*does* exist'. **insignibus insignis,** 'notable as the deeds are notable'. **luella,** 'atonement': the word is not found elsewhere.

1016. **saxo**: the Tarpeian rock on the Capitoline Hill, about 80 feet in perpendicular height, from which criminals were thrown to their death. **deorsum**: here scanned normally *de-or-sum*.

1017. With this list of nouns cf. V. 1192 (extract no. 29). **robur**: either (*a*) 'dungeon', i.e. *Robur Tullianum*, the lowest dungeon of the Mamertine Prison at Rome; or (*b*) 'rack'. **lammina**, 'the branding iron'.

1018. **at**, 'yet', introducing the main clause after a concessive clause. **mens . . . conscia**, 'the guilty conscience'. **sibi** with *adhibet*: 'applies to itself'. **factis**: dat. with *praemetuens*: 'fearing for its misdeeds'.

1019. **torretque**: sc. *se*, understood from *sibi*, 'and sears itself'.

1022. **eadem . . . haec** and **magis** belong in the *ne* clause.

1023. 'In short, the life of fools becomes a hell on earth': *hic* 'here (on earth)' as in 992; *Acherusia* 'hellish'. By *stultorum* is meant, of course, those who are not Epicureans: the Stoics used exactly the same word to describe those who disagreed with them.

20. Sensation the Basis of all Perception (IV. 26–43)

26–29 summarize the contents of Book III.

26. **esset**, 'is': after 'I have shown' the Eng. idiom demands a present, but the Latin perfect indicative is nearly always treated as an historic tense, even when equivalent to the Eng. perfect with 'have'. Similarly render *vigeret* and *rediret* as present.

27. **compta**: cf. I. 950 n. (extract no. 7). **vigeret**, 'grows'.

28. **quove** = *quoque*: cf. I. 57 n. (extract no. 2). **ordia prima**: see 'Style', p. xxv.

29. **agere**, 'explain'. **vementer**: see 'Metre', p. xxx.

30. **simulacra**: see n. on III. 433 (extract no. 16).

31. **membranae**, 'films'. **summo . . . corpore**, 'surface'.

32. **ultroque citroque**, 'to and fro'.

33. **vigilantibus . . . atque in somnis**, 'waking and sleeping'. **mentīs**: acc. plur.

35. **contuimur,** 'behold': from *contuor* (3), a collateral form of *contueor*: see 'Language', p. xxvii. **luce carentum,** 'of those who have lost the light of day' (Bailey). These 'images of the dead' were thrown off by the persons concerned during lifetime. The bundles of atoms making up these images do survive, but not the individual human beings from whom they emanated.

36. **horrifice** : with *excierunt*. **sopore** : with *languentis*.

37. **exciĕrunt.** The shortening of the *e* in this form was probably a colloquial pronunciation. Its convenience to the poet is obvious (cf. p. xxvi, l. 24), and it is found in Plautus and Terence, but Lucr. appears to have been the first to permit it in hexameter verse. **ne . . . reamur** depends on *agere incipiam* (29). **Acherunte** : as in III. 978 (extract no. 19).

40. **simul** : adv. with *perempta*. **atque** joins *corpus* and *animi natura* (= *animus*). **perempta** : neut. plur. qualifying *corpus atque animi natura*; the use of the neut. plur. to refer collectively to non-personal nouns of mixed gender is regular.

41. **discessum dederint** = *discesserint*: see n. on *dat* I. 288 (extract no. 6).

42. **effigias** : another synonym for *simulacra* and *imagines*. For *effigia*, an archaic form of *effigies*, cf. *materiem* I. 58 n. (extract no. 2).

43. **mittier** = *mitti*.

21. Optical Illusions (IV. 379–403)

379. **hilum** : cf. III. 830 n. (extract no. 17).

380. **quocumque,** normally relative, is here interrogative and introduces a reported question: 'in what several spots there is light and shade'.

381. **illorum est,** 'it is their function'. **eadem,** etc.: sc. *utrum* here and again in the next line, 'but (whether) they are the same lights or not, and (whether) the shadow . . .'.

383. **paulo** : with *ante* in the *quod* clause. 'What we said a little before' was that the lights and the shadow are not the same, but that stationary points of light dying out in front, and new points of light

coming into being behind, give the impression of the shadow moving.

384. **hoc**: see 'Metre', p. xxix. So also in 386. **animi demum ratio,** 'only the reasoning of the mind'.

386. **proinde**: see 'Metre', p. xxx. **adfingere,** 'falsely impute'.

387. **qua vehimur navi** = *navis qua vehimur*: cf. *ea quae . . . corpora* II. 134 n. (extract no. 10). **fertur**: cf. *ferri* II. 84 n. (extract no. 9).

388. **in statione,** 'at rest'. **praeter . . . ire**: tmesis.

390. **quos . . . praeter,** 'past which'.

391. **cessare**: as in II. 80 (extract no. 9). **cavernis,** 'vaults'.

392. **et,** 'and yet', as *-que* III. 1004 (extract no. 19). **assiduo . . . motu**: abl. of description, but tr. '*in* constant motion'.

393. **longos** (= *longinquos*) **obitus,** 'distant settings'. **revisunt**: see n. on *revisit* II. 359 (extract no. 12).

395. **videtur**: the MS. reading: for the singular number cf. *sentit* III. 843 n. (extract no. 17).

396. **in statione**: as in 388. **ea**: neut. plur. in apposition to *sol et luna*, cf. *perempta* IV. 40 n. (extract no. 20); tr. 'bodies' or omit. **res . . . ipsa,** 'actual fact'.

397. This whole line belongs grammatically after *quos* in the next line, but is placed first for emphasis, as being the topic of the whole sentence; *exstantis . . . montis* are acc. plur. governed by *inter* with *quos* as an adj. in agreement: cf. Verg. *Aen.* I. 573 *urbem quam statuo, vestra est.* This is another instance of the idiom already exemplified in *qua vehimur navi* 387 n. etc.: in English 'mountains' would be the antecedent—'a single island seems (to be formed) from mountains etc., between which there is a gap' etc. However, the Latin order can be preserved by not too violent an anacoluthon: 'And mountains standing up . . ., between which . . . —these nevertheless seem to unite to form a single island.'

398. **classibus**: with *patet exitus*.

400. This line belongs in the clause *uti . . . videantur* (401), which is a noun clause subject of *fit* ('it happens that . . .'); the result

clause 'signposted' by *adeo* begins in 402 (*vix ut* . . .). A literal tr. would begin with *ubi* (401): 'When children have themselves stopped spinning round, it comes about that the rooms seem to them to revolve and columns fly round, so much so that they can now hardly believe . . .'. Note the imitative effects here: the alliteration in this line (see 'Style', p. xxiv) and the rapid dactylic rhythm of the next.

402. **desiĕrunt**: from *desino*. For the short *e* cf. *excierunt* IV. 37 n. (extract no. 20).

403. **ruere**, 'to fall in'. A prolative infinitive is not found with *minor* outside Lucr., who frequently extends this usage to verbs with which other writers do not use it: cf. *praeripere* III. 896 n. (extract no. 18).

22. Sensation the Basis of all Knowledge (IV. 469–84)

469. **denique**: not 'lastly' but 'and then', introducing a new topic. This is the primary meaning of the word. **id quoque . . . an sciri possit**, 'whether that can be known either' (i.e. his belief that nothing can be known). A single question introduced by *an* is usually to be regarded as the second part of a double question, with the first part suppressed, e.g. III. 868 n. (extract no. 17). Here, however, we see the survival of a usage common in early Latin of *an* as a simple interrogative, equivalent to *num* introducing a reported question.

470. **scire**: sc. *se*.

471. **hunc**: governed by *contra*. **mittam contendere causam**, 'I will refrain from joining issue': *mitto* with infinitive ('forbear to . . .') is not uncommon in Cicero.

472. 'who deliberately stands on his head', i.e. stands self-convicted of topsy-turvy reasoning.

473. **hoc quoque uti concedam**, 'to grant even this'. **scire** (sc. *eum*) explains *hoc*, 'that he *does* know' (whether it can be known that nothing is known). **at**: as in III. 1018 (extract no. 19).

475. **unde**: we say 'how'. N.B. *ŭn-dĕ scĭ-*: Lucr. has several in-stances of a final short open syllable before a word beginning with a combination of *s* and another consonant. Later poets (except Horace in the *Satires*) generally avoided it.

476. **notitiam**: see n. on *notitiai* II. 124 (extract no. 10). **veri . . . falsique**, 'of the true and the false'.

477. **dubium certo . . . differre**, 'that the doubtful differs from the certain'.

478. **primis ab sensibus**, 'from the senses as its origin'.

479. **notitiem**: another noun of which Lucr. uses 1st or 5th decl. forms indiscriminately—cf. I. 58 n. (extract no. 2) and IV. 42 n. (extract no. 20).

480. **maiore fide . . . illud**, 'something of greater reliability'. **reperirier** = *reperiri*.

481. **veris**, like *falsa*, is neut. plur. **quod possit**: relative clause of result, 'such that it can'.

482. Sensation is the basis of all our knowledge. This is the bedrock of the Epicurean theory of knowledge, as we have tried to show in the introduction to Book IV.

483. **an** introducing a reported question was met in the first sen-tence of this extract (see n. on 469) and in III. 868 (extract no. 17). A direct question introduced by *an* frequently urges acceptance of a proposition involved in the preceding sentence, which is commonly a question also: tr. 'Or . . .?', 'Then . . .?' Cf. Terence *Ad.* 781, *non manum abstines? an tibi iam mavis cerebrum dispergam hic?* 'Are you not going to keep your hands off? Or would you rather have me scatter your brains over the place now?' The first question 'expects' the answer 'yes': the second is a strong incentive to the person addressed to give that answer. So here the *an*-question urges acceptance of the proposition, implied in the preceding question, that *nothing* is more trustworthy than the senses. **falso**. Lucr. uses the word his opponents apply to the senses: *if* the senses are false, can reason, which springs from them, be used to con-tradict them? **ratio**: see n. on I. 51 (extract no. 2); here 'reason', 'reasoning'. **valebit** = *poterit*.

484. **eos** is governed by *contra* and refers to *sensibus* following.

23. Images in Sleep (IV. 1011–23)

1011. **porro,** 'moreover'. In the passage immediately preceding this extract, Lucr. had described the behaviour of animals in their sleep, which suggested that they were dreaming of their waking activities: the same, he now says, applies to human beings. **motibus :** i.e. the movements of the mind-atoms. **edunt magna,** 'bring forth mighty deeds'.

1013. **reges expugnant,** 'subdue kings'. It gives better sense to take *reges* as acc. than nom.: to a Roman, kings were generally enemies. A personal object with *expugno* is unusual, but not unparalleled. **proelia miscent,** 'join battle'.

1014. **si** is superfluous. A clause of 'unreal' or 'ideal' comparison is in origin a condition with suppressed apodosis: 'they cry out as (they would be doing) if they were being murdered'. By the conditional tense-rule we should expect *iugularentur,* but the rule of sequence takes precedence (*a*) regularly if 'as if' is a single word in Latin (e.g. *mandantur* 1017), (*b*) exceptionally if *si* appears as a separate word, as here. **ibidem :** with the main verbs, 'all without moving'.

1015. **depugnant :** a technical term for gladiatorial combat, 'fight in the arena'. **doloribus :** abl. of cause.

1017. **mandantur :** from *mando* (3), 'devour'.

1019. **indicio . . . sui facti . . . fuere,** 'have borne witness to their own misdeeds': *indicio* predicative dat., *facti* objective gen. instead of the second dat. normal with a predicative dat.

1022. **exterruntur :** from *exterro* (3), a collateral form of *exterreo*; see 'Language', p. xxvii. **mentibu' capti,** 'insane': for the meaning of *capio* cf. n. on I. 941 (extract no. 7).

1023. **aestu,** 'disturbance'.

24. The Imperfection of the World (V. 195–234)

195. **quod si iam . . . ignorem,** 'but even supposing I did not know' (as I do). There are several instances in Lucr. of *si* with a present instead of the normal imperfect subjunctive to express an untrue supposition about the present time. In III. 843 (see n., extract no. 17) *si iam* introduced a supposition, equally untrue in Lucretius' opinion, in the present indicative. Here the main verb is

present subjunctive, and this influences not only the mood, but also the tense, of the verb in the *si*-clause. **primordia,** like *exordia* II. 333 n. (extract no. 12), may be nom. or acc.

196. **rationibus,** 'workings', as in I. 54 (extract no. 2). **ausim,** 'I would venture'. This archaic form, in origin an aorist optative, was used as an alternative present subjunctive of *audeo* by poets of all periods: *faxim* is also quite common, and *prohibessit* has been mentioned in the n. on III. 444 (extract no. 16).

197. **reddere,** 'prove': short for *rationem reddere* (cf. I. 59 n., extract no. 2), 'render an account', and so 'account for' a fact.

198. **divinitus:** cf. I. 150 n. (extract no. 5). **paratam,** 'created'.

199. **stat** = *est*, cf. *constant* II. 337 (extract no. 12), etc. Many forms of the verb 'to be' in the Romance languages are derived from *sto*. **culpa,** 'imperfection'.

200. **quantum . . . inde,** 'of all that . . .'. **impetus,** 'expanse'; Latham's 'sweep' is felicitous, paralleling Lucretius' application to size of a word primarily suggesting violent motion.

201. **avidam partem,** 'the greedy half'; by a rather violent hypallage, 'greedy' means 'appealing to greed'. Some editors emend *avidam* to *avide* or *avidi*.

204. **inde . . . porro,** 'besides'. **duas . . . partis,** 'two-thirds', i.e. the tropical and arctic zones.

205. **geli casus,** 'fall of frost'. Lucr. uses *gelum -i* n.: the normal form is *gelus -ūs* m.

206. **arvi,** 'arable land'. N.B. *suā vi*.

211. **subigentes,** 'working'. **cimus ad ortus,** 'summon (the crops) to birth': *cio* (4) was the original form of the verb normally found as *cieo* (2), e.g. V. 1060 (extract no. 28).

212. **nequeant:** the crops are the understood subject. Note the irregular form of the condition, with present indicative in the protasis and present subjunctive in the apodosis.

213. **quaesita** is the subject of *frondent*, 'things won . . .': again crops are meant.

215. **aetherius sol:** see 'Metre', pp. xxxii–xxxiii.

216. **peremunt,** 'destroy': from *peremo*, the original spelling of *perimo*.

221. **vagatur,** 'stalks abroad'.

222. **tum porro,** 'then again'. **puer,** 'child', cf. I. 936 n. (extract no. 7). **ab** may be 'from' or 'by': see n. on III. 429 (extract no. 16).

223. **navita:** see 'Language', p. xxvii. **infans,** 'speechless': the primary meaning of the word. **indigus** here with abl., more often with gen.: e.g. II. 650 (extract no. 14).

224. **vitali,** 'necessary to life'. **in luminis oras:** cf. I. 22 n. (extract no. 1).

227. **cui . . . restet:** causal relative clause, 'since . . . is in store for him'. **tantum . . . malorum:** see n. on I. 101 (extract no. 4); *tantum malorum* is the object of *transire*, 'to pass through such a deal of woe', the whole phrase forming the subject of *restet*.

228. **pecudes armenta,** 'flocks and herds': cf. *ferae pecudes* I. 14 n. (extract no. 1), but here the two words in asyndeton refer to tame beasts, and *ferae* is joined to them by *-que*.

229. **crepitacillis,** 'rattles'.

230. 'a foster-nurse's fond baby-talk': *infracta*, 'broken', i.e. disjointed, inarticulate.

231. **pro tempore caeli,** 'to suit the season'.

233. **qui,** 'with which'. This old form of the abl. sing. after a plur. antecedent is found elsewhere in Lucr. and also in Plautus.

234. **daedala rerum,** 'the artificer of things': cf. I. 7 n. (extract no. 1).

25. How the World Arose (V. 416–31)

416. **ille . . . coniectus,** 'that gathering together' (which you see).

417. **fundarit:** perfect subjunctive of *fundo* (1), 'established'. The spondees give this and the next line a majestic sound. **ponti . . . profunda** = *pontum profundum*: cf. *prima virorum* I. 86 n. (extract no. 4).

418. **ex ordine,** 'in order'.

420. **suo** monosyllabic: see 'Metre', p. xxxi.

421. **quos quaeque darent motus:** reported deliberative question, 'what movements each should start'. With *darent* cf. *dat* I. 288 n. (extract no. 6). **pepigere:** *pango* (cf. I. 24 n., extract no. 1) has three perfects: (i) *pegi*, 'I fixed'; (ii) *panxi*, 'I composed'; (iii) *pepigi*, 'I made a bargain'. Present-stem forms of the verb are used only in the first two meanings, *paciscor* supplying the third.

423. **percita**, 'driven on', not 'set in motion'. The original motion of the atoms is caused by their own weight, as mentioned in the next line; the 'blows' of the other atoms merely determine the direction of the motion. **plagis**: cf. *ictu alterius* II. 85 (extract no. 9).

424. **consuerunt**, (*con-svē-runt*) 'have been accustomed'. The perfect of *consuesco* has the force of a present (cf. n. on *suemus* I. 60, extract no. 2), but here it is the 'present which includes the past', for which the Eng. idiom demands the perfect: cf. Cic. *Cat.* I. 12 *te iam dudum hortor*, 'I have long been urging you'. **ferri**: cf. II. 84 n. (extract no. 9).

425. **omnimodis** = *omnibus modis*, apparently coined by Lucr. on the false analogy of *multimodis* (e.g. III. 856 n., extract no. 17).

426. **inter se**: with *congressa*. **possent**: for the tense, cf. *esset* IV. 26 n. (extract no. 20). The attribution, which this subjunctive implies, of purpose to the atoms in a passage expressly written to refute the idea of purposive creation appears to be inconsistent. It is worth noting, however, (i) that the inconsistency really lies in the use of *pertemptare* in the previous line: after a verb meaning 'try' a subjunctive of purpose is only logical; (ii) that Lucr. also uses a purpose clause in VI. 693 (extract no. 32) when describing volcanic activity—as if natural phenomena themselves had the purpose of proving to humanity their own causality! So we say 'the facts speak for themselves' without really being conscious of personification.

427. **vulgata**, 'scattered abroad'.

428. **omne genus**, 'of every kind': internal acc. qualifying *coetus* and *motus*, which are acc. plur. **experiundo**: see 'Language', p. xxvii.

430. **exordia**: here in the ordinary sense of 'beginnings', not 'atoms'. **saepe**: since our world is only one of many so formed.

26. Early Man (V. 925–61)

925. **illud**, 'of that time'.

926. **quod** introduces a causal relative clause, 'seeing that . . . it'.

927. **solidis magis** = *sŏlĭdĭoribus*, which would be impossible in an hexameter.

928. **fundatum**, 'built': cf. *fundarit* V. 417 (extract no. 25). **aptum**, 'fitted': cf. *apti* III. 839 n. (extract no. 17). **viscera**, 'flesh'. **nervis**, 'sinews'.

929. **quod** = (*tale*) *ut id*. Take *quod* first and *facile* with *caperetur* (result subjunctive): 'not likely to be easily harmed by either heat or cold'. With *ex* cf. *a* III. 429 n. (extract no. 16); for the meaning of *capio* cf. I. 941 n. (extract no. 7).

930. **labi**, 'ailment': abl. (normally *labe*).

931. 'and during many lustres of the sun rolling through the sky': *lustrum* = a period of five years; *volventia* intransitive, as *depellere* II. 219 n. (extract no. 11).

932. **vulgivago**, 'widely roving': a Lucretian coinage not found elsewhere. **tractabant**, 'dragged out': frequentative of *traho*, which commonly has this meaning. The more usual sense of *tracto* is found below, l. 953.

934. **quisquam**: adjectival with *moderator*, 'any steerer'. **nec scibat**: sc. *quisquam*, 'nor did anyone know'. For the form *scibat* see 'Language', p. xxvii. So also in 949, 953, and 959. **molirier** = *moliri*: 'how to work':

935. **defodere**, 'plant'.

937. **quod**: antecedent *id donum* in the next line.

939. **curabant corpora**: see n. on II. 31 (extract no. 8).

940. **quae . . . arbita**, 'the arbutus berries which . . .': cf. *ea quae . . . corpora* II. 134 n. (extract no. 10); *arbitum* (more often *arbutum*) = the fruit of the arbutus or wild strawberry.

942. **plurima . . . etiam maiora**, 'in great abundance (and) also of larger size (than now)'.

943. **novitas . . . florida mundi**, 'the flowering youth of the world'.

944. **ampla** here, unusually, means 'ample', 'sufficient'.

945. **sedare . . . vocabant**, 'invited them to quench'. The use of the infinitive with *voco* is poetical: cf. *ruere* IV. 403 n. (extract no. 21).

946. Cf. I. 283 (extract no. 6).

947. **claricitat late**, 'loudly summons from far and wide'. This is Lachmann's emendation of the MS. *claricitati a te*. If it is correct, *claricito*, which is found nowhere else, must be the frequentative of *clarigo* (or *clarico*), although the simple verb is never transitive;

for its meaning see Lewis & Short, s.v. *clarigatio*. The same meaning is given by Forbiger's *claru' citat late: clarus* meaning 'loud', transferred from the sound itself to what makes it, is unusual but paralleled by Verg. *Aen.* VII. 141–2,

> *hic pater omnipotens ter caelo clarus ab alto intonuit* . . . .

948. The subject is again primitive men, as in 939. **nota vagis :** sc. *sibi*, 'familiar to them in their wanderings'. **silvestria templa tenebant,** 'they would inhabit the woodland haunts': see n. on II. 8 (extract no. 8).

949. nympharum : see commentary on extract no. 1, p. 10.

950. See 'Style', p. xxiv. **lubrica,** 'gliding', with *fluenta*. **lavere :** collateral 3rd conj. form of *lavare*: see 'Language', p. xxvii.

951. umida saxa : cf. *aurea* III. 13 n. (extract no. 15). **super :** as in I. 65 (extract no. 3). **viridi . . . musco :** local abl., 'over the green moss'. **stillantia** agrees with *fluenta*.

952. partim, 'here and there'. **plano . . . campo :** local abl., 'over the level plain'. **scatĕre** (collateral 3rd conj. form of *scatĕre*) depends, like *lavere*, on *scibant*: 'welled up'. Note again the 'reinforcement' of an unusual grammatical form.

953. res . . . tractare, 'to serve their purposes' (lit. 'handle things').

955. colebant = *incolebant*.

956. squalida, 'rough' from exposure.

958. commune bonum . . . spectare, 'look to the common good'.

960. quod . . . praedae, 'whatever booty' (= *id praedae quod*).

961. sponte sua sibi : with *valere et vivere*, 'at his own will for himself (alone)'. **valere,** 'thrive'.

27. The Growth of Civilization (V. 1011–23)

1012. It is virtually certain that between 1012 and 1013 a line has dropped out which contained, among other words, (i) a noun with which *unum* agrees (e.g. *coniugium*), (ii) a conjunction (since the *postquam* clause continues to *creatam*), (iii) the subject of *cognita sunt* (e.g. *iura*): tr. 'retired to a single (union, and the laws of marriage) were learnt'.

1015. **curavit** = *effecit*, 'brought it about'. In prose only persons can be the subject of *curo*. **alsia**, 'cold': *alsius -a -um* (from *algeo*, as *noxius* from *noceo*) is found nowhere else, but Cicero twice uses *alsius* as a neuter comparative, as if from *alsus*, which is otherwise unknown.

1016. **ita**, 'so well' (as before).

1017. **Venus**: see p. 10, footnote 3. **pueri**: cf. I. 936 n. (extract no. 7). **parentum** depends on *ingenium*.

1018. **blanditiis**, 'by their winning ways': cf. *blanda* V. 230 (extract no. 24). **fregere**, 'broke down'.

1019. **amicitiem** = *amicitiam*: cf. *notitiem* IV. 479 n. (extract no. 22) etc. **aventes**, 'longing': on this depend *nec laedere nec violari*.

1020. **inter se**: with *iungere*.

1021. **commendarunt**, 'commended to one another's care'. **muliebre . . . saeclum**, 'womenfolk'. N.B. *mu-li-ēb-re*.

1022. Bailey takes the subject of *significarent* to be the children, and *balbe* to mean 'in broken words'—of a child just learning to speak. It seems, however, doubly unlikely (*a*) that *significarent* should have a different subject from *commendarunt* with no pronoun to indicate the fact, (*b*) that if it were so, the new subject should be only half of the object of *commendarunt*. We prefer to think that the men are still the subject of *significarent*, and that *balbe* means 'inarticulately'—referring to the fact that the human race is just learning to speak (see the next extract). Why should it be left to the children to draw their elders' attention to their responsibilities?

1023. **imbecillorum . . . misererier** (= *misereri*) **omnis**, 'for all to pity the weak'; noun phrase subject of *esse*, which is the infinitive of the reported statement after *significarent*.

28. The Origin of Language (V. 1028–61)

1028. at marks the transition to the next topic. **subegit** = *coegit*: but with *subigo* in this meaning, unlike *cogo*, the infinitive is unusual; cf. *ruere* IV. 403 (extract no. 21) etc.

1029. expressit, 'shaped', 'fashioned': a metaphor from sculpture.

1030. non alia longe ratione atque, 'very much as', lit. 'in a manner not far other than'; *atque* as in II. 351 (extract no. 12).

1031. protrahere, 'lead on'. **infantia,** 'speechlessness': cf. *infans* V. 223 n. (extract no. 24).

1032. facit = *efficit*, 'causes' them to . . . . **quae sint:** relative clause of result, 'such things as are'.

1033. sentit . . . vis . . . suas quoad possit abuti, 'feels to what purpose he can use his own powers', lit. 'feels his own powers, to what purpose he can use (them)': *vis* acc. plur. as in II. 586 (extract no. 13). This is another instance of the idiom explained in the note to I. 949 (extract no. 7), with the difference that if the phrase *vis suas* had been placed in the reported question, it would have been abl. governed by *abuti*. N.B. also that *quoād* is monosyllabic by synizesis, and that *abuti* here has its primary and commoner meaning 'use to the full', not 'misuse' as in II. 656 (extract no. 14).

1034. Begin with *prius quam*. **nata . . . exstent,** 'sprout and grow out': Lucr. here follows the Greek usage of subjunctive in all future temporal clauses rather than the Latin usage of indicative unless there is an idea of purpose as well as time. **vitulo:** cf. *omnibus* I. 19 n. (extract no. 1). **frontibus:** tr. as sing.

1035. illis = *cornibus*, as if they were there. **petit,** 'butts'. **infestus,** 'aggressively' (Latham). **inurget,** 'pushes'.

1036. catuli, 'cubs'. Strictly the diminutive of *catus* ('cat'), the word is used for the young of any animal. **scymni:** see 'Language', p. xxviii; tr. 'whelps'.

1038. vix etiam : with *creati*.

1039. alituum, 'of winged things': see 'Language', p. xxviii.

1040. **auxiliatum** = *auxilium*: see 'Language', p. xxvi.

1041. **putare . . . prima**: this whole phrase is the subject of *est* (1043).

1042. **inde,** 'from him'.

1043. **desiperest,** 'is folly': *desipere* 'to be foolish'. **cur hic posset**: past deliberative question, 'why should this man have been able . . .?'

1045. **tempore eodem alii . . . putentur**: present deliberative question, joined to *hic posset* etc., by asyndeton, with *cur* still operative, '(and) at the same time others be thought . . .'.

1046. **usi . . . fuerant** = *usi erant*. For the indicative in a supposition which the writer regards as untrue see n. on *si iam* III. 843 (extract no. 17). The whole sentence could have been expressed *nisi alii . . . usi essent, notities non insita esset . . .*; but Lucretius' rhetorical questions make a far more emphatic apodosis, and since they are necessarily indicative, so is the protasis.

1047. **insita . . . est**: sc. *huic* from the next line. **notities**: see notes on II. 124 (extract no. 10) and IV. 479 (extract no. 22).

1049. **quid vellet facere**: object of *sciret* and *videret*. **scirēt**: see n. on *fulget* II. 27 (extract no. 8).

1051. **poterat,** 'would not have been able' (sc. even if he had wished). An unfulfilled possibility in the past is stated in Eng. conditionally, but in Latin usually absolutely—i.e. by the indicative, not subjunctive: cf. Plautus, *Mil.* 911, *bonus vates poteras esse*, 'you might have been a good prophet'.

1052. **docere**: sc. *surdos*; wilfully deaf is meant of course. **suadere**: see n. on I. 101 (extract no. 4).

1053. **quid sit opus facto,** 'what needs to be done'. The abl. sing. neut. of the perfect participle with *opus est* is normal usage. Duff explains *quid* as acc. of respect, but it may be nom., as if *opus facto* were *faciendum*: cf. n. on II. 20 (extract no. 8). **neque enim paterentur,** 'for they would not endure it' (sc. if anyone were trying to teach them).

1054. **sibi . . . amplius auris . . . obtundere,** 'to batter on their ears for very long': in a negative sentence, where we say 'not very', Latin uses the comparative.

1055. **inauditos**: either '(previously) unheard' or 'unintelligible'.

1056. **mirabile tantopere**, 'so very remarkable': cf. *amari tanto opere* III. 909 n. (extract no. 18), but here, instead of a partitive gen., the adj. agrees with *quid*. N.B. *tántòperést rè*.

1057. **cui . . . vigeret**: causal relative clause. The sequence is taken from *notaret* in the next line.

1058. **pro vario sensu varia . . . voce**, 'with diverse sounds to express diverse feelings'. **notaret**, 'should have distinguished'. The use of the subjunctive is contrary to the general principle quoted in the note to *si iam* III. 843 (extract no. 17), and to Lucretius' own practice with expressions like *quid mirum si . . . ?* Moreover the use of the imperfect is contrary to the rule of sequence. Both irregularities may perhaps be explained by the argument that Lucr. has transferred to this expression what would have been the regular mood and tense in a past deliberative question, to which the whole sentence is equivalent: i.e. *cur non notaret?* 'why should it not have distinguished?' Alternatively, it is possible that Lucr. wrote *notavit* and that the scribe, influenced by *vigeret* at the end of the previous line, inadvertently altered this to *notaret*.

1059. **cum**, 'since': lines 1059–60 form a causal clause loosely attached to the preceding sentence. **denique**, 'even'.

1060. **ciere**, 'utter'.

1061. **dolor**, 'pain'. **gliscunt**, 'swell', 'grow strong'.

29. The Origin of Religion (V. 1161–93)

1161. The structure of the first sentence is as follows: 1161–3 form a reported question depending on *rationem reddere* (1168); 1164 and 1165 are both relative clauses with *sacra* (1163) as antecedent; 1166–7 is a relative clause with *horror* (1165) as antecedent; 1168 is the main clause.

1162. **ararum**, 'with altars'. Cicero too uses a gen. with *compleo*, but the abl. is commoner.

1163. **curarit**: meaning as in V. 1015 n. (extract no. 27), though with a different construction. **sollemnia**, 'annual'. **sacra**: here scanned *săc-ra*.

1164. **sacra**: here scanned normally *să-cra*; omit in tr., cf. Caesar, *B.G.* I. 6. 1, *erant omnino itinera duo, quibus itineribus exire possent.* **rebu'** = *rebus publicis*: 'states', 'empires'. **locisque**: sc. *magnis* again, 'and at great places' such as Rome itself.

1165. **etiam nunc**: this was certainly true of the Oriental cults to which reference has been made on p. 3, even if it had ceased to be true in Lucretius' day of the official religion.

1166. **suscitat**, 'raises'. **orbi**: abl., normally *orbe*: cf. *labi* V. 930 (extract no. 26).

1167. **cogit celebrare**, 'makes (men) throng (them)'.

1168. **non ita**, 'not very'. **rationem reddere**: cf. I. 59 n. (extract no. 2).

1169. **quippe etenim**, 'for indeed'. **iam tum**, 'even then'. Lucr. returns to primitive times after his reference to contemporary religion in 1164–7. **divum**: with *egregias facies*. **mortalia saecla**, 'the races of mankind'.

1170. **animo . . . vigilante**: abl. absolute, 'when the mind was awake', i.e. in trances or day-dreams. Earlier in Book V (148 sqq.) Lucr. explains that the gods are composed of such fine atoms that they give off only the thinner type of surface-film (see n. on III. 433, extract no. 16), which cannot be apprehended except by the mind.

1171. **et magis in somnis**, 'and still more so in sleep'. **mirando corporis auctu**: with *facies; auctus*, 'bulk'.

1172. N.B. *próptèreá quòd*.

1173. **videbantur**, 'were seen' rather than 'seemed'.

1174. **pro**, 'to match', 'befitting'.

1175. **dabant** = *tribuebant*: sc. *homines dis*.

1176. **suppeditabatur**, 'kept recurring'. **manebat**, 'remained unchanged'.

1177. **et tamen,** 'and apart from that', introducing an alternative reason true 'in any case' (*omnino*), i.e. even if the reader were to dispute *quia . . . manebat.* **auctos** (sc. *deos*), 'endowed'.

1178. **non temere,** 'not easily'. **convinci** = *vinci*. This is the only instance in Lucr. of *convinco* in this sense. For the use, now obsolete, of Eng. 'convince' = 'overcome', see *O.E.D.*

1179. **fortunis,** 'in happiness'. **ideo:** with *putabant.* **praestare:** sc. *deos sibi.*

1180. **vexaret:** subjunctive because the clause is expressed as a reason for *praestare* in men's thoughts, whereas *quia . . . videbant* is expressed as a reason for *putabant.* The meaning of *timor . . . vexaret* could have been expressed as *timorem . . . vexare videbant.*

1181. **in somnis:** with *videbant* in the *quia* clause.

1182. **efficere:** sc. *deos.* **et,** 'and yet', as in IV. 392 n. (extract no. 21). Here *ipsos* emphasizes the contrast.

1183. **rationes,** 'workings', as in I. 54 (extract no. 2) and V. 196 (extract no. 24). N.B. *rationes* is one object of *cernebant*, the acc. and inf. phrase *tempora verti* ('that the seasons come round') another.

1185. **nec poterant . . . cognoscere** is the main clause.

1186–7. 'Therefore they took refuge in attributing everything to the gods and making everything be governed by their will' (lit. 'they considered it a refuge for themselves to hand over . . . and to make . . .'). This sense of *facio* with acc. and inf., 'represent' in word or thought, i.e. 'assert' or 'suppose', is not uncommon in prose: e.g. Cic. *Tusc.* IV. 35, *poetae impendere apud inferos saxum Tantalo faciunt.* Eng. 'make' is similarly used.

1188. **templa:** see n. on II. 8 (extract no. 8).

1189. **videtur** agrees only with its nearest subject: it has fifteen altogether, nine of them plural; cf. *sentit* III. 843 n. (extract no. 17). See also 'Style', p. xxiv.

1190. **severa:** Duff tr. 'austere', denoting the coldness and purity of the stars, and quotes Keats, *Hyperion* I. 74, 'the earnest stars'.

1191. The 'night-wandering brands' and 'flying flames' are meteors and comets.

1192. Cf. III. 1017 (extract no. 19).

1193. 'and the rapid roars and mighty rumbles of menace.'

30. True Piety (V. 1194–1203)

1194. **genus**: acc. of exclamation, cf. *mentis . . . pectora* II. 14 (extract no. 8).

1195. **cum tribuit**, 'to attribute' or 'in attributing'. An historic indicative is regularly used in a *cum* clause which denotes an action identical with that of the main verb: e.g. Cic. *Rosc. Am.* 39, *de luxuria purgavit Erucius, cum dixit hunc ne in convivio quidem ullo fere interfuisse*, 'E. cleared my client of the charge of riotous living, in saying . . .'. The present instance is complicated by the fact that there is no main verb, the *cum* clause depending on an acc. of exclamation. But the usage is the same: men's attribution of such acts to the gods constituted their *infelicitas*, just as the statement of the prosecutor Erucius about the accused Roscius constituted his (unintended) *purgatio* of the man.

1196. **ipsi sibi**, 'for *themselves*': *ipsi* is rendered in the emphasis on 'themselves'.

1197. **peperere**: cf. *peperit* I. 83 n. (extract no. 4). **minoribu'**, 'descendants'.

1198. **velatum** = *operto capite* and agrees with the understood subject of *videri*, '(for a man) to be seen, with veiled head, to turn . . .'.

1199. **vertier** = *verti*. **lapidem** may be a sardonic description of the idol as a 'thing of stone', or it may be the boundary-stone (*terminus*), which was considered sacred and often anointed or crowned.

1202. **quadrupedum**: scanned *quād-rŭ-pĕ-dum*. **votis nectere vota**, 'link prayer to prayer', i.e. utter one prayer after another.

1203. **sed mage**, 'but rather (true piety is) . . .'; *mage* for *magis* (via *magi'*): so *amabere* for *amaberis*. **pacata posse omnia mente tueri**: *ataraxia*.

31. Thunderbolts (VI. 379–99)

380. perspicere, 'the way to view'. **rem quamque** is the object of *faciat* ('each thing'—i.e. 'whatever it does'), the whole clause *qua . . . quamque* being the object of *videre*.

381. Tyrrhena . . . carmina: these particular Etruscan books, which contained the methods of divination by lightning are mentioned by Cic. *De Div.* I. 33. **retro volventem,** 'unrolling': *volventem* agrees with the understood subject of *perquirere*, '(for a man) to seek out'.

383–6. These reported questions are loosely placed in apposition to *indicia*, although they are matters of observation, not inquiry: in tr. supply 'observing . . .'.

383. utram appears to be used for metrical reasons in place of *quam*: for purposes of divination, the sky was divided not into two, but into sixteen parts, and the significance of the lightning was determined by observing from which part it arose and into which it disappeared. Note the rhythm of the last two feet *aút ìn utrám sè*, repeated in 385 *éxtùlerit sè*.

384. hinc: i.e. from earth. The thunderbolt was believed to strike the earth and then disappear into the sky again. **partim:** the original acc. sing. of *pars*, used as such by Cicero and Livy as well as Lucr., and as an adv. by writers of all periods. **quo pacto,** 'how': cf. I. 84 n. (extract no. 4), but there *quo* is relative, here interrogative.

385. et hinc dominatus ut extulerit se, 'and how, after playing the tyrant, it rose up hence'.

386. quid: internal acc. with *nocere*, 'what harm the stroke . . . can do'. The pollution of the spot is meant, not material damage.

388. templa: see n. on II. 8 (extract no. 8).

389. quo . . . cumque: tmesis; so also *quibus . . . cumque* in the next line.

390–1. The construction is very involved: *cur non faciant ut* ('why do they not bring it about that'—cf. V. 1032 n., extract no. 28) *quibuscumque est incautum scelus aversabile* ('whoever have not refrained from some abominable crime'—lit. 'to whomsoever there

s unguarded-against a crime to-make-a-man-turn-away') *icti
flammas fulguris halent* ('(are) struck (and) reek-of the flames of
lightning'). Here Lucr. uses *fulgur* for *fulmen*.

392. **documen . . . acre,** 'a sharp lesson': internal acc. in apposition
to the preceding *ut* clause.

393. **et potius,** 'and (why) rather': *cur* (390) is still operative, cf. V.
1045 n. (extract no. 28). **nulla sibi turpi conscius in re,** 'one
with no foul deed on his conscience'.

394. **inque peditur** : see 'Style' p. xxv.

395. **turbine . . . et igni** : hendiadys, 'fiery whirlwind'. **subito** :
probably adv.

397. **an** : as in IV. 483 n. (extract no. 22). Here the *an* question
urges acceptance of the proposition, implied in the preceding
questions, that thunderbolts are not instruments of divine vengeance. **consuescunt** is transitive: 'accustom', 'practise'.

398. The subject, when last mentioned (387), was *Iuppiter atque
alii divi*, but now must clearly be *alii divi* only.

399. **parcit in hostis,** 'keeps it (for use) against his enemies'.

32. The True Explanation of Volcanic Eruption
(VI. 680–702)

681. **foras,** 'forth', 'abroad'.

682. **subcava,** 'hollow underneath'.

683. **fere,** 'everywhere': cf. II. 370 n. (extract no. 12). **silicum
. . . cavernis,** 'by arches of basalt'. **suffulta,** 'supported': from
suffulcio.

684. **aer** : scanned *ā-ēr*. The word is borrowed from Greek, in
which *a* and *e* do not form a diphthong. In oblique cases and derivatives the *e* is short: e.g. *āĕris, āĕrius*.

685. **ventus enim fit** etc. : *ventus* is the complement of *fit*, *aer*
the subject: 'air becomes wind'. (Without the comma after *percitus*,
ventus would be the subject of *fit*: 'wind is created when air' etc.)
This is the only passage in which Lucr. speaks of wind as simply air
in motion: elsewhere he regards wind and air as distinct entities,

although closely akin. For instance in I. 271–81 (extract no. 6) air is not mentioned. **agitando**, 'by agitation'.

686. **hic**: see 'Metre', p. xxix.

687. **qua contingit**, 'wherever it touches them'. **terram**: soft earth as opposed to rock. **ollis**: see 'Language', p. xxvii.

688. **excussit**, 'has struck out', as iron does from flint.

689. **se**: object of both *tollit* and *eicit*. **rectis . . . faucibus**: abl. of route, 'straight through the crater': cf. *rectum per inane* II. 217 n. (extract no. 11). **eicit**: pronounced *ē-ji-cit*: see 'Metre', p. xxix.

693. **ne dubites**: see n. on *possent* V. 426 (extract no. 25). **animai**, 'of the wind'. The form of the Greek *anemos* (ἄνεμος), 'wind', appears in the Latin *animus*, but its meaning was assigned to the collateral form *anima*. From this primary meaning the other senses of *anima* are derived.

694. **magna ex parti**, 'in a great degree'. For *parti* as abl. cf. *labi* V. 930 (extract no. 26), *orbi* V. 1166 (extract no. 29), and also the acc. *partim* VI. 384 (extract no. 31).

695. **aestum**: the 'backwash' of each wave, not 'tide': the Mediterranean is almost tideless.

696–7. 'From this sea caves reach underneath (*subter*) right up (*usque*) to the crater at the top.'

697–8. It seems certain that a line has been lost between 697 and 698. Bailey favours the suggestion *fluctibus admixtum ventum, quem surgere saepe*, giving the meaning: 'By this path it must be admitted that there enters (wind mingled with the waves, which) the-nature-of-the-case (*res*) compels (to rise often) and penetrate deeply from the open sea . . .'.

701. **crateres** is the Greek word for bowls in which wine and water were mixed: the population of Sicily was to a large extent of Greek descent and Greek-speaking. Note that the short *e* of the Greek 3rd decl. nom. plur. is retained—*crātērĕs*: cf. *lampadas* II. 25 n. (extract no. 8).

702. **quod**: sc. *id*, in loose apposition to *crateres*, '—that which we call . . .'.